Bibliographic information published by the German National Library:

The German National Library lists this publication in the National Bibliography; detailed bibliographic data are available on the Internet at http://dnb.dnb.de .

Imprint:

Copyright © 2018 GRIN Verlag
Print and binding: Books on Demand GmbH, Norderstedt Germany
ISBN: 9783668890251

This book at GRIN:

https://www.grin.com/document/455215

Haitham Ismail

How to utilize the IaaS cloud safely? Developing cloud security for cloud adoption in the Middle East

GRIN Verlag

GRIN - Your knowledge has value

Since its foundation in 1998, GRIN has specialized in publishing academic texts by students, college teachers and other academics as e-book and printed book. The website www.grin.com is an ideal platform for presenting term papers, final papers, scientific essays, dissertations and specialist books.

Visit us on the internet:

http://www.grin.com/

http://www.facebook.com/grincom

http://www.twitter.com/grin_com

DISTANCE LEARNING THROUGH ARDEN UNIVERSITY (RDI)

IN PARTIAL FULFILMENT OF THE REQUIREMENTS FOR THE DEGREE OF

MSC INFORMATION SYSTEMS (SYSTEMS SECURITY)

Dissertation

Developing cloud security for cloud adoption in the Middle East

SUBMITTED BY (HAITHAM ISMAIL)

Abstract

Information Security is very important to business and national security of any country. In the Middle East, especially with the current geopolitical tensions and unbalance situation resulting from terrorism raising, cyber security is very important to protect nation's economy and security. This research investigates with a deep look inside hybrid cloud security deployments, which is new to Middle East region with focusing on Infrastructure as a service security (IaaS). Besides, it assesses the current practice when it comes to cloud data adoption in an IaaS environment. whether it is on-premises or hosted by a third party, dedicated or shared across multitenant. This research is to develop two templates to be followed by IT professionals whether they had the required expertise for cloud adoption or not to guide them through the whole data cloud adoption process. According to the risk appetite of the organization and their acceptable risk level, the template is chosen. These templates contain a guide to design the cloud security infrastructures, the placement of information in different IaaS deployment models (e.g. private IaaS, public IaaS, community IaaS, etc.), and what controls recommended to establish controls and governance in the cloud realm. These templates were developed based on the recommendation and guidelines National Institute of Standards and Technology (NIST), Cloud Security Alliance (CSA), and European Union Agency for Network and Information Security (ENISA).

Table of Contents

List of tables

Keywords

Cloud Computing; Cloud Security; Private Cloud; Public Cloud; Cloud Security Strategy; Infrastructure as a Service security; IaaS; hybrid Cloud

1.0 Chapter 1: Introduction

Cloud computing is a new terminology that has been noticed in the IT World recently. It is considered as a new trend of emerging technologies that invade the world in general. However, There is a potential for growth in utilizing cloud services. Furthermore, business is becoming agiler than ever, which means that the ability of business to respond quickly to market changes efficiently (VMware, 2011). Cloud Computing gives IT the required agility for business to perform better to market changes. According to Cisco Global Cloud Index (2016), the Middle East and Africa cloud traffic are expected to be in growth from 69 Exabyte in 2015 to 304 Exabyte in 2020. In fact, everybody uses cloud computing technology with knowledge or without knowledge. People are using cloud services through their smartphones daily. For example, if a mobile application is downloaded from internet store to a smartphone, then a user starts taking a photo, editing them and storing them, so these are cloud services that have been used. Furthermore, over 120 hours of video is being uploaded every min; emails are daily exchanged by millions. These are considered examples of Cloud services too that became available to the public during the past decade (Mint, 2016). It is considered an approach for providing IT services from a third party whether it resides on-site or off-site customer premises with opportunity for a broad, scalable, and broad Network Access (Mell and Grance, 2011). It's most important benefit is offering its services by the low cost that is affordable and easy to access (Ruboczki and Rajnai, 2015). It can be described as offering on-demand IT services that are used by individuals, enterprises and governments over the internet with automatically provisioning resources. Famous examples are Microsoft Online, Gmail, Online CRM, Google Apps, 3Tera AppLogic, Amazon EC2, Skype for Business, OneDrive, etc. (Alali and Yeh, 2012). The first thing to think about when adopting data in the cloud is how much this data is protected in the cloud space.

However, not all cloud consumers are aware of the risks associated with data cloud adoption, But still using it as users upload thousands of gigabyte per day to cloud (Mint, 2016). Robinson et al (2011) argue that one of these risks might be a loss of governance on the data and application that resides on a third party network by which cloud consumers do not have full control over it, and this will have a direct impact on Security triad confidentiality, integrity and availability. Furthermore, the risk associated with cloud security adoption is higher in the Middle East Countries, a senior information security consultant Suleman (2016) argues that the geopolitical tensions and chaos status in the region bring more security challenges to the cloud adoption in these countries, therefore their data in cloud will become valuable targets of cyber-attacks from cyber criminals, terrorists and government. Besides, there is a risk associated with adopting data in the cloud as the resources are shared with the public that which brings privacy challenges, and clients have no controls over the infrastructure (Gaurav and Shuchi, 2016).

1.1 Aims and Objectives

The main aim of this paper is guiding the information technology (IT) professionals in the region to utilize infrastructure as a service (IaaS) cloud's benefit in a hybrid deployment model through a safer approach that will be achieved by working on the following objectives:

Objective 1:

Critically evaluate existing literature review related to cloud architecture and its security infrastructure including all publications from National Institute of Technology (NIST), European Union Agency for Network and Information Security (ENISA), and Cloud Security Agency (CSA) with concentration over (IaaS) service model.
Objective 2:

Conducting user engagement approach in the Middle East countries to identify current cloud security posture for cloud consumers in the Middle East by getting their thoughts about their state of cloud adoption and identify risks associated it.

Objective 3:

Prepare a template for designing IaaS cloud security infrastructure especially for IaaS. These templates will help in guiding IT professionals to utilize cloud services, set the design for cloud security infrastructure and select the security defences to protect data in the cloud.
Objective 4:

Offering the template to a sample of IT Professionals to check their feedback on how their confidence in cloud computing is affected if they use this strategy.

In this research, Only two template has will be developed, one for the low-risk appetite organizations that accept a low level of risk, and the other one is for high-risk appetite organization that accepts a high level of risks. The organizations that can accept a level of risk in between are not the audience of this research.

8

1.2 Brief Outline

This paper will begin with a critical evaluation of existing literature review related to cloud computing and IaaS security. This will help in the understanding of the research's topic and latest research findings. Following that, research methods that are used in this paper will be discussed, and how these methods will be used. These methods are a literature review, observations, interviews, and surveys. Data collected through all of these methods was used through a methodological triangulation validation method to validate and confirm the findings of different stages of the research. Chapter 4 discussed the observations of the author about the research topic. However, experts interviews were discussed in chapter 5. Based on the data collected through literature review and observations, confirming and validating the results will be from data collected through the interviews methods. In chapter 6, the organizations was classified based on their risk appetite. Following that, the template was derived to guide these organization to guide in the cloud security adoption.

In chapter 7, a survey was conducted to assess, validate and confirm chapter 6 findings. And finally, the last chapter was summarized the research activity and tries to link the market future with the research finding.

2.0 Chapter 2: Literature Review

Information technology (IT) professionals try every day finding a new way to serve business objectives. In today world, there are needs to business that IT is trying to match. For examples, delivery of IT services with lower running cost, interact with dynamic needs of business, and availability. Cloud computing is a new terminology that is raised in the hall of IT recently that can satisfy these needs. It is a new model or method of delivering IT resources over the internet; it is a resource that varies from storage, computing power to application and software (Haeberlen and Dupre, 2012). Even home users start to use it with knowledge or without their knowledge of the term cloud computing, and they post videos and photos to YouTube, Flicker, and Facebook (LaGesse, 2009).

2.1 Cloud definition and Characteristics

Mell and Grance (2011) state that Cloud Computing is a model of enabling convenient on-demand access to a shared pool of self-managed configurable resources such as Network, servers, storage, and applications that are rapidly provisioned, accessed broadly and can be measured. It has main characteristics such as the following:

- On-demand Self-service: cloud user can get cloud benefits based on his needs without human interaction, for example, the consumer can schedule provisioning of the resources within their peak time only and de-provision them later automatically (Krutz and Vines, 2010).
- Broad Network access: Cloud services are available from anywhere over a different kind of links whether these links are internet or WAN or fibre or Microwave (Mell and Grance, 2011).
- Rapid Elasticity: or in another word, quickly scalable based on demand up and down (Krutz and Vines, 2010).
- Resource Pooling: the cloud computing whether it is physical and virtual resources are shared across multi-cloud users that dynamic assigned based on the cloud user needs (Mell and Grance, 2011).
- Measured service: the resources of that are used by the tenants are changing with time; however, it is monitored, metered, controlled and reported in a transparent manner (Krutz and Vines, 2010).

The mentioned characteristics can be restated in more critic way by saying that it is the technology that enables the consumer to lower their starting cost. This lowering of cost is achieved due to one of cloud's main characteristics which is resource sharing. The concept of sharing IaaS resource allows the consumer to get the benefit of high tech technology, starts quickly and procuring cloud computing with the minimum possible amount of investment. Cloud computing is built upon a software of virtualization that gives consumers the ability to have on-demand control over the resources within the shared resources without the need of interacting of a third party that increases the level of trust and decrease the time taken for adding more resources when compared with traditional IT. Also, cloud computing has a broad access feature that indicates that the location of the provided services is not important except for monitoring the legal risk in the services provided country. Besides, it is an independent platform by which it can be accessed through mobile, laptop, windows platform, Unix platform, etc. Finally, the provided services is controled, monitored and measured. For example, the used resources (e.g. storage) by a consumer are dynamically changed with time on-demand. The used storage is monitored and based on the occupied space on the storage consumer will pay or pay as you use payment model.

2.2 Cloud service models

A cloud infrastructure is considered as a collection of hardware and software that provides the previously mentioned characteristics of cloud computing. Cloud services are available through three services model. First, Software as a Service (SaaS) is providing cloud consumer (CS) applications that are running on the cloud infrastructures. CS uses thin clients or web browsers to access these applications. Furthermore, CS does not have control over the underlying infrastructure such as storage, servers, OS, etc. (Haeberlen and Dupre, 2012).

Second, Platform as a Service (PaaS) is providing the CS with the ability to deploy his application based on languages, libraries, and tools supported by the CSP, nevertheless, CS does not control the underlying infrastructure of networks, servers, storages, other network resources and of course securing all of this component (Mell and Grance, 2011). Finally, Infrastructure as a service (IaaS) is providing the CS the abilities to self-provision processing, storage, network, servers (e.g. Virtual Machines.) which can make him able to run applications from the cloud. Furthermore, unlike the previously mentioned service models, IaaS consumer is responsible for all the underlying infrastructure from storage, servers, operating systems, etc. (Haeberlen and Dupre, 2012).

However, Blokland et al (2013) statues that there are four main building blocks that build cloud-computing space.

- Application: Software/application that runs in the cloud (e.g. CRM, OneDrive, Gmail)
- Platform: Runtime environments that depend on tools, programming languages and libraries (e.g. dotNet, PHP, ASP, etc.)
- Virtualization: Virtual copy of device whether it is network or servers gives the ability to provide multiple version of the device that is quickly provisioned on demand (VMware servers, virtual firewalls, virtual intrusion prevention, etc.)
- Hardware is the physical elements that will carry the virtual environments that are the backbone cloud computing capabilities (e.g. blade servers, cables, racks, firewalls, switches, etc.)

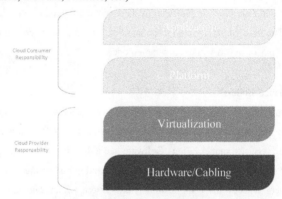

Figure 1 - Four main building blocks of cloud computing (IaaS responsibility distribution)

Blokland, et al (2013) state that the responsibility of the management of these blocks (See Figure 1, Page 12) is shared between providers and consumers. In IaaS, CSP has the responsibility of managing the low-level infrastructure (Hardware & Virtualization) and their security. CSP has the physical security responsibility including building fences, managing gates, air condition, CCTV, an environmental monitor, access control to the datacenter etc. Besides, visualization components that include as an example hypervisor, network manager security, etc. While the CS has the responsibility of managing and securing platforms (e.g. Windows servers,) and the applications running on top of it. Consumer security measure includes patch management, vulnerability management, secure coding of custom applications, etc.

2.3 Cloud deployments model

According to Mell and Grance (2011), there is four deployment model that cloud consumers use when thinking to adopt their data to the cloud.

- Private Cloud: the entire cloud infrastructure is reserved exclusively for single cloud tenant that is managed by the consumer or a third party. It might be located on or off premises
- Public Cloud: Cloud infrastructure is shared among multi-tenants (business, academic, governments, etc.). it is located in the cloud provider premises.
- Community Cloud: Cloud infrastructure is shared among tenants shared same concerns. It can be located on or off premises.
- Hybrid Cloud: it is a combination of public, private and community cloud computing.

Most of the consumers are using a combination of these deployment model. Organizations has to select the suitable deployment model for each type of data they own. For example, an insurance company that has an enterprise-owned datacenter can have a backup site (disaster recovery site) that is hosted on a cloud provider (Private cloud). besides, its development team can use some development machines that are hosted on Mircosoft Azure (Public). Because of regulations, all healthcare sector must share medical records the government through a datacenter hosted in a government facility (Community cloud), All of this can be considered a pure example of hybrid cloud deployment model.

2.4 Cloud benefits

Cloud computing gives Infinite computing resources available that are on-demand and quickly provisioned enough to follow load surges. Besides, business can start small and increase hardware & software when they have business growth. CS can release when the resources are no longer in use. In addition, it is considered as a way to convert capital expenses to operating expenses. In fact, it plays important role in decreasing the information technology cost, and it decreases the risk of over-provisioning or under-provisioning.

Usually, CSP has a large scale cloud network infrastructure, so the same amount of investment in security and can provide better protection for the consumer. In addition, CSP can offer to hire the required expertise that can work on and manage specific security situations and have better threat management capabilities, therefore CSP can provide consumers with the latest better security technology by lower prices (Haeberlen and Dupre,

2012). Besides, Cloud computing market is considered as a cutting-edge market by which CSP is doing their best to have a good reputation in the market and attracting more consumers, therefore they are more than welcome to have the latest security controls and be the best market differentiator (Alassafi et al., 2017). CSP can quickly reallocate resources for filtering, bandwidth management, encryption and other security controls to support mitigation of attacks such as distributed denial of service DDOS. Besides, multiple consumers are using cloud resources for the same CSP which give him the visibility about the latest market attacks trends (e.g. Phishing campaign, malware outbreak, etc.), that will help him better protecting his consumer. In addition, the consumer can have the right to audit that can be written in a service level agreement to enhance risk management (Haeberlen and Dupre, 2012).

2.5 Risk Management Framework for Cloud Ecosystem
However, adopting data in the cloud is assosiating with many risks. In general, risk is a function of the probability that negative outcomes occurred and the value of this outcome (Iorga and Karmel, 2015). Managing these risks requires a framework (See Figure 2, Page 22) that will discipline the activities that are integrated to all aspects of the organization from planning system development life cycle SDLC to security & privacy controls allocation, operation and monitoring (ISACA, 2011). In this Framework, Cloud Consumer (CS) needs to perform risk assessments that will assess the information processed, transmitted and stored based on business impact analysis to identify and analyze the risks associated with cloud adoption. Besides, CS identifies the security requirements for cloud-based services and he prepares risk treatment plan. Following that, he selects risk-adjusted security and privacy controls or asking for customizing controls in the CSP infrastructure. For example, CS is responsible for securing data in the cloud echo system until the hypervisor level (see Figure 1, Page 17). Besides, CS must identify the best suitable cloud-based architecture, identify security and privacy controls that are needed. In addition, CS must select the cloud partner, analyze his security posture, define and negotiate cloud-based SLA as well as (See Figure 2, Page 22) implement CS controls and authorize the cloud-based information system to operate. Finally, CS must monitor the effectiveness of the controls implemented (Iorga and Karmel, 2015).

2.6 Cloud Associated Risks

Haeberlen and Dupre (2012); Armbrust et al (2010); Alassafi et al (2017); Vaquero et al (2011) help in identifying risks by stating that some these risks[1] can be illustrated in the following point.

Threat 1. Data Lock-in: data cannot be extracted and migrated to another vendor CSP that increase the risks to the price increases.

Threat 2. Loss of Governance: CS will lose control over the underlying infrastructure as he will host his data to a third party (e.g. CSP), so it has direct impact on confidentiality, availability and integrity

Threat 3. Malicious insider: CSP employees have responsibility That is completely separate from CS (e.g. CSP system administrator), so they have high privilege on CS infrastructure

Threat 4. Insecure data deletion and shared resources issues: the resources are scaling up and down, so it has a high probability of data exposure due to ineffective data deletion.

Threat 5. Issue raising due to sharing the resources: it is unauthorized access to information due to share of resources

Threat 6. Management interface compromises or account Hijacking: it is internet accessible and it is subjected to vast of attacks from hackers that might use any known or unknown vulnerability to have unauthorized access.

Threat 7. Abuse use of cloud computing: using IaaS for hosting botnets, Trojans, etc.

Threat 8. Insecure APIs: API can manage and interact with the cloud services.

---

1 Threat n will be used later during the literature review and discussion

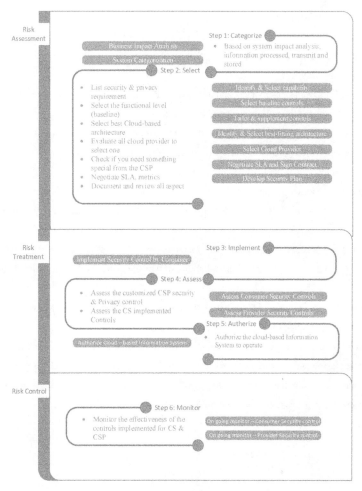

Figure 2 - Risk Management Framework for cloud Echo-system

2.7 IaaS Security

Infrastructure as a service (IaaS) is the ability to provide the consumer with the required processing, storage, networks, and other fundamental computing resources (Mell and Grance, 2011). IaaS cloud has the same security concern as traditional it and more due to sharing the resources with other tenants. IaaS consumer does not share only the physical host, also it shares the network resources links and network interfaces by virtualization (Vaquero, et al.,

16

2011). Furthermore, CSP has no control over the hypervisor level (See Figure 1, Page 17), so once the VM is infected, VM share the same physical host can attack each other (Gordon, 2015). Gonzales et al (2015) state that a trust zone must be created. Trust zone (TZ) (See Figure 3, Page 17) is a collection of network segmentation and identity access management (IAM) servers that use usernames, access control list (ACL) and active directory to control access to cloud resources. A TZ is dedicated to a single tenant, and its Security can be enhanced by only permitting preconfigured MAC address and IP address to connect to IAM servers. The security depends on the right configuration of the firewall, switches, active directory, etc. if it is misconfigured then it is introducing a vulnerability.

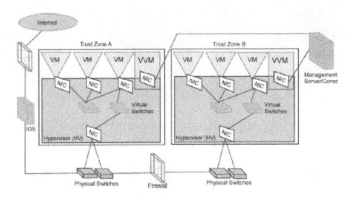

Figure 3 - an example of separation between trust zones (Gonzales et al., 2015, p 524)

However, the cloud infrastructure management traffic, security-monitoring traffic, IAM server and VM traffic are not separated, so the surface of infection increase risk (e.g. VM to VM, VM to the hypervisor, etc.) which is categorized as collocation attack (Gordon, 2015).

Gonzales et al (2015) introduce, based on Defense information system agency (DISA) recommendations, a new reference architecture model and that completely separate (See Figure 4, Page 24) the cloud management traffic from VM cloud for each tenant. CSP Management traffic is filtered and isolated through CSP TZ firewall, while CSP security and monitoring servers are isolated and monitored through CSP Enclave firewall. Besides, CS security and monitoring servers are isolated by firewall as well.

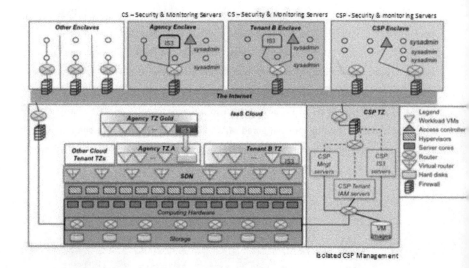

Figure 4 - enhanced security cloud reference architecture model (Gonzales et al., 2015, p525)

Through the previously mentioned architecture model, all management, security and monitoring traffic of different cloud actors acting on the cloud are isolated through firewalls.

2.7.1 VM Security

As mentioned, the backbone of the cloud technology is visualization, and it is subjected to the threats that were mentioned earlier (See Table 1, Page 19). Therefore, securing the VM in all its life cycle plays an important rule for securing cloud IaaS. Vaquero et al (2011) state that VM image files should be encrypted in transit or storage. In fact, it is protected by using HTTPS, SSH, TLS with mutual authentication between the VM and its controller (hypervisor) that will work on adapting the VM to its future environment. Trusted based mandatory access control technology will be used to block any abnormal behaviour from its expected baseline (Raj and Schwan, 2009 cited inVaquero, et al., 2011).

Life cycle name	Potential threats	IaaS infrastructure dependencies
Transportation	Threat 1, Threat 5, Threat 8	Shared network
Storage	Threat 1-5, Threat 7-8	Shared Network, storage

Deployment	Threat 3, Threat 7, Threat 8	Shared Hypervisor, Network, storage
Contextual	Threat 1-3, Threat 5-8	Shared Datacenter, Hypervisor, Network, storage,
Runtime	Threat 1-3, Threat 5-8	Shared Datacenter, Hypervisor, Network, storage
At Rest	Threat 1-3	Shared Datacenter, Hypervisor, Network, storage
Deletion	Threat 2, Threat 3, Threat 4, Threat 8	Shared Storage, Hypervisor, Network, storage

Table 1 - Threats affecting the VM during its life cycle

2.7.2 Hypervisor Security

Virtual Machine Monitor (VMM) or hypervisor main purpose is to monitor and manage the VM that it is running on the hypervisor. Obasuyi and Sari (2015) state that the visualization layer or the host operating system level is separating (See Figure 5, Page 20) the hardware resources from the VM. Vaquero et al (2011) state that the fact of the guest machine is a VM should be hidden from attacker detection. Normally, attackers detect that he is in a VM environment by detecting the host and guest OS, Communication channel detection, or memory differences as the location of the Interrupt, global and local distributor table varies between host OS and VM OS.

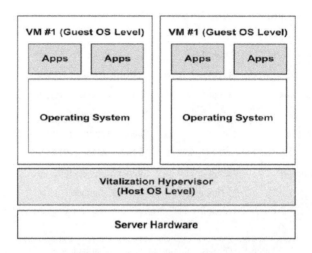

Figure 5 - Virtualization Architecture (Obasuyi and Sari, 2015, p261)

2.7.3 Datacenter Security

It depends on the secure platform (e.g. Trusted Platform Module TPM) which is a combination of hardware and software, and its main objective is to provide isolation of the process. TPM is not designed to be accessed by multiple devices in the same time, so IBM introduced virtual TPM that allow all guest VMs can communicate to have its own separated TPM (Vaquero, et al., 2011).

2.8 Countermeasures

In addition, Gonzales et al (2015) state four cloud arch model with different security controls to be introduced to enhance IaaS cloud infrastructure (See Table 2, Page 21) such as VM image encryption at rest, multi-factor authentication for the CSP IAM servers, VM Isolation and Tenant IAM servers authentication type. In addition, Signed Hypervisor and signed BOIS is used for mutual authentication between the VM and its hypervisor. Furthermore, the isolation is implemented on many layers such as VM Isolation, Network Isolation, CSP monitoring, management, and security traffic network isolation (See Figure 5, Page 18) and CS management, monitor and security traffic network isolation.

	VM Images At Rest	VM Migration	CSP Sys-admin IAM	Data Center physical security	Hypervisor, BIOS, CPU	VM Isolation	Tenant IAM	App. White-listing
Cloud Arch 1	Not encrypted	Unencrypted memory pages and packets	Single factor	All CSP employees have access	HV, BIOS not signed CPU without TPM	No network, CPU isolation	Single factor	No
Cloud Arch 2	Not encrypted	Unencrypted memory pages and packets	2 factor—time limited token code	CSP employee access limited & controlled + USB server ports disabled	HV, BIOS not signed CPU without TPM	No network, CPU isolation	Single factor	No
Cloud Arch 3	Not encrypted	Unencrypted memory pages and packets	2 factor—time limited token code	CSP employee access limited & controlled+ USB server ports disabled	HV, BIOS not signed CPU without TPM	No network, CPU isolation	2 factor—time limited token	No
Cloud Arch 4	Encrypted at rest + file access monitoring	Encrypted memory pages and packets	2 factor—time limited token code	CSP employee access limited & controlled+ USB server ports disabled	Signed HV, signed BIOS CPU with TPM	Virtual PANs, temporal CPU isolation	2 factor—time limited token	Yes

Table 2- Cloud Reference architecture model (Gonzales et al., 2015,p526)

He et al (2014) argue that the firewall can be placed like traditional IT. Information Security specialists have three option to place the firewall within the cloud (See Figure 6, Page 21).

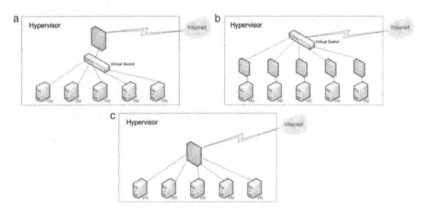

Figure 6 - Firewall deployment options (He, et al., 2014, p. 118)

First, one virtual firewall inside the hypervisor (See Figure 6a, Page 27) which will consume hypervisor's resources. However, if any virtual machine VM infected, it can attack another machine hosted behind the firewall. Second, a dedicated virtual firewall (See Figure 6b, Page 27) is introduced for each VM. In such scenario, the security level increases as protection and logical isolation are provided for each VM, but it consumes huge resources from the hypervisor. Finally, one virtual firewall for all VMs (See Figure 6c, Page 27) so that the firewall protect and logically isolate all VM, so it will provide protection and consume fewer resources.

2.9 Service level of Agreement (SLA)

It is very important for the cloud adoption process, and typical one is a contract between the service provider and a consumer to define a description service provided, responsibility of each one of the two parties, cost, monitoring, reporting of the service level and penalties of not meeting the SLA (PaloAlto Network, 2017). However, Cloud SLA is deferent; there are more parameters to be added to the SLA such as data protection policies that will include how data will be protected, preserved, accessed, transferred, processed and purge (Gordon, 2015). Furthermore, an agreement of transparency in case of security breach notifications. Finally, disaster recovery and what is the incident response steps and responsibilities and the associated disruption (Hausman, et al., 2013).

2.10 Conclusion

Cloud Computing has many benefits that will help facilitate information technology work in enterprise now a day, but, it adds different kinds of risks on the top of what traditional IT has.

These risks can be managed in a systematic approach or a framework, which is published by the national institute of standard and Technology (NIST) under a name of risk management framework for cloud echo system (RMF4CE). RMF4CE has the following steps

- Risk Assessment: it is based on business impact analysis for the information created, processed, transmitted, stored, and destroyed.
- Risk Treatment: Assess CSP Infrastructure and choose controls and implemented for cloud consumer (CS)
- Risk control: monitor all controls and SLA.

Infrastructure as a service (IaaS) is one of the cloud service models that can be protected by separating the cloud service provider (CSP) from CS traffic. In addition, separate CS management, security, and monitoring traffic from normal VM traffic. On the other hand, the same is applied for CSP.

Gonzales et al (2015) worked hard to set a cloud architecture reference model that cover all the weak points when utilizing IaaS service model. However, their paper talked about IaaS's security apart from the deployment model used (e.g. Public IaaS, Private IaaS, hybrid IaaS, community IaaS). Besides, there is no information about the recommended security and monitoring controls to be used in the different kind of deployment models.

3.0 Chapter 3: Research Methodology

In this paper, a combination of research methods such as literature review, observations, interviews, surveys and methodological triangulation validation will be used to answer research questions. They will be used in a sequence (See Figure 7, Page 30) to validate the finding of the research findings and develop the adopting strategy. The method will select to achieve the previously mentioned objective (See Table 3, Page 23).

Step No.	Method	Objective
1	Literature review: critically evaluate the existing literature.	Objective 1
2	Observations: collect data for the threat model and security controls used in the to protect the infrastructure against these threats	Objective 2
3	Experts interviews: experts will validate and confirm observation findings	Objective 2
4	Literature review: information from latest literature conducted in step 1 and last step findings will be used to prepare a cloud adoption strategy or framework in IaaS environment.	Objective 1
5	Surveys: information collected will validate the effectiveness of the strategy or framework and communicate the overall research findings to the community.	Objective 4
3,5	Methodological triangulation validation: validate the finding to verify achieving objectives	Objective 2 & 3 & 4

Table 3 - Method Objective Matrix

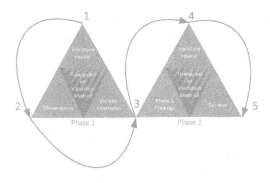

Figure 7 - Methodological triangulation validation sequence

3.1 Observation Research Methods.

First, observation research method is considered as a qualitative research method that is used for data collection without interacting with the research environment (Williamson, 2000 citied in Baker, 2006). It permits the researchers to study phenomena or an environment and its surrounding media by recording their observation about the observed topic in a systematic approach (Groman and Clayton, 2005 citied in Baker, 2006). In our scenario, observation method will enable the researcher to observe and record the threat model associated with cloud adoption. In another word, it will record what the cloud adoption's threats, current practice mitigating controls, and administrative controls are. Furthermore. Observation will be conducted based on literature reviews and experience in the field.

3.2 Interviews Research method

Second, Interview is a qualitative research method, which is a dialogue between two or more persons with the aim to collect information relative to a research topic. It enables the researcher to work directly with the participants to get more clarity on answering the research questions (Wilson, 2012). It will be used within this paper for validation of the findings from the observation research method by asking open-ended questions to give the participants to express the reason behind their answers when validating the observation results (Alassafi et al., 2017). However, Beck & Manuel (2008) state that the following steps should be performed in order to have successful interviews

- Identify the participants: a participant is considered as an expert if he has five years of experience or more in the information technology field. The participant are selected from different working field such as insurance, government, IT, etc. The interviews will be conducted for five information technology experts from the Middle East countries.
- Select the interview type (personally, by telephone, Skype, etc.) and the type will be selected based on my reachability to them and their time and availability.
- Select the location to conduct the interview in
- Test the devices that will be used to conduct the interview with (Such as recorders, smart phone, PC, etc.).
- Design the interview questions and its schedule
- Obtain a formal consent.
- Conduct the interview.

- Write its transcript

3.3 Surveys Research method.

Third, Surveys are a quantitative research method used for gathering information from entities and to identify aspects of the research topic by asking questions on the sample and record their answers for further analysis. Groves et al (2009) state that open-end and closed-end questions are the most common type of questions used in this research method.

3.3.1 Open-ended questions:
- All participant are asked to express their answers in their own words.
- It is usually to identify and explain the reasons behind the experts.

3.3.2 Closed-ended questions:
- Participants are choosing their answers from predefined choices.
- Answers should include all possible answers and meaning should not overlap.

The order of the questions presented should be considered, and sensitive questions (e.g. income, gender, etc.) should not be included. Beside, double-barreled questions which are asking two questions in one and biased words should not be used. It will be conducted through electronic (e.g. Google analytics) or paper surveys

In this research, it will be used to confirm the strategy developed from the other research methods. In addition, linking the research with the market to validate its effectiveness.

3.4 Methodological triangulation validation

Methodological triangulation research method is the use of research method collections (more than 1) to study a research topic, for example, data can be collected by observation method and open-ended interviews (Casey and Murphy, 2009 cited in Bekhet & Zauszniewski, 2012). it is normally used for providing validation and confirmation of data, and it provides more comprehensive data that will help in enhancing understanding the topic (Bekhet & Zauszniewski, 2012). In addition, it is used to decrease the disadvantages of a method and strengthen the finding of the research (Denzin, 1978 citied in Bekhet & Zauszniewski, 2012). It will be used in this research (See Figure 7, Page 30) to validate the finding of the Literature review and observation by conducting expert's interviews as a first step. Then, information from the last step and Literature review interview will be validated and confirmed with Surveys.

4.0 Chapter 4: Observation

4.1 Observation Findings and data analysis.

As known, observation is recording of all the factors affecting the research topic and it will be done based on literature review and personal experience in the field.

4.1.1 Expected growth:

- Cloud datacenter growth is expected to be in growth (See Figure 8, Page 32) from (21% 259) in 2015 to (47% 485) in 2020 (Cisco, 2015, p. 4).

- The dependency on traditional datacenter will be declined (See Figure 9, Page 35) from 60.9% to 46.2% (Cloud Security Alliance, 2017a, p. 8).

- All type of cloud deployment model is expected to be in growth (See Figure 9, Page 35) (Cloud Security Alliance, 2017a, p. 8).

- Scaling up & down is the first motive behind cloud adoption (See Figure 10, Page 27), Then, and cost saving (Cloud Security Alliance, 2017a, p. 9).

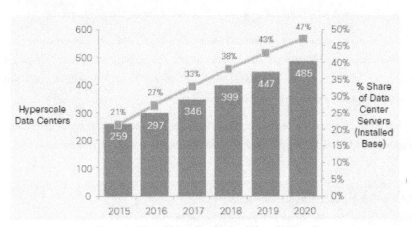

Figure 8 - Cisco Global Cloud Index (Cisco, 2015, p. 4).

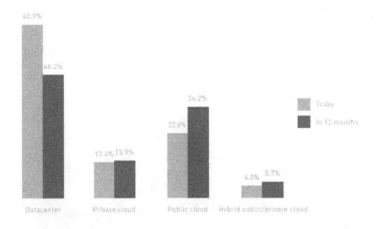

Figure 9 - the expected growth of deployed by Infrastructure type (Cloud Security Alliance, 2017a, p. 8).

Figure 10 - Reasons behind that expected growth (Cloud Security Alliance, 2017a, p. 9).

Data collected through observation phase highlight the importance of cloud computing in the future. There are is an expected growth (See Figure 8, Page 32) in the hyperscale datacenter numbers that are located all over the world in a five years' time window (Cisco, 2015). The growth will be from 259 hyperscale datacenters in 2015 to 485 hyperscale in 2020. The expected growth, geographic locations (See Figure 11, Page 36), and geopolitical tension in the region might make Middle East countries to attract a number of this expected datacenters to be built in their territories taking in consideration that most of the submarine cables are passing through their soil. Therefore, Enterprise is gradually intending to move their environment (e.g. testing & Production) to cloud. The number of enterprise-owned data centres (See Figure 10, Page 35) is expected to be dropped from 60.9 percent to 46.2 percent, and most of this growth is expected to be in Public cloud deployment by (Cloud Security Alliance, 2017a).

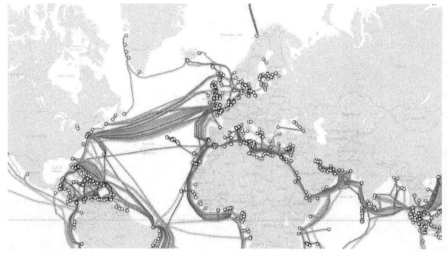

Figure 11- Submarine Cables in the Middle East (Submarine Cable Map, 2018)

Therefore, this is of necessity that will raise the need and the attention to cloud security. Normally, the attraction to cloud computing (See Figure 10, Page 35) due to its major benefits scalability & cost saving, and this is a direct result of the cloud computing 's characteristics rapid elasticity and resource pooling (Krutz and Vines, 2010).

4.1.2 Responsibilities of parties:

According to Cloud Security Alliance (2017b), the respondents was divided based on the following.

- In IaaS environment, Cloud security provider (CSP) has the responsibility to (See Figure 12, Page 29):
    o Physical Security of cloud datacenter.
    o Cloud Security Infrastructure.
- Cloud Consumer (CS) is responsible for (See Figure 12, Page 29):
    o Data security and its classification.
    o Endpoint protection.
    o Identity and access management.
    o OS and application level security.
- Network Security is shared responsibility.

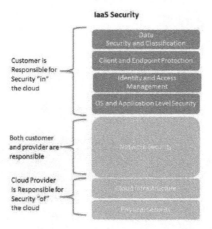

Figure 12 - the responsibility distribution between CS & CSP (Cloud Security Alliance, 2017b, p. 10)

In IaaS service model, CSP has the responsibility of the physical security and cloud infrastructure (See Figure 12, Page 37). CSP has the responsibility to build a security process to protect the physical security of the data center including policies, procedures and controls such as fences, CCTV, cooling, power regulation, device management, etc., besides, cloud infrastructure or host security such as Storage, VM manager or hypervisor, etc. (Microsoft, 2018).

Although it is a pure responsibility of CSP, CS must keep the physical layer and cloud infrastructure (host) security under his radar. CS is at the risk of CSP malicious insider[2]

CS can protect himself by good SLA that include for example the right to audit the CSP, access to CCTV, access to logs of CSP identity access management, security monitoring logs, etc. Besides, it has penalties and contracts termination circumstances. Cloud network security is a shared responsibility between both parties (See Figure 12, Page 29). They need to cooperate to make sure that the network access control and storage are configured in a secure manner. CS has the pure responsibility for Data security and its classification, client and endpoint protection, OS and application layer security such as OS or application patching (Cloud Security Alliance, 2017b, p. 10).

---

2 Threat 3 from Literature review

4.1.3 Cloud Protection Scheme.

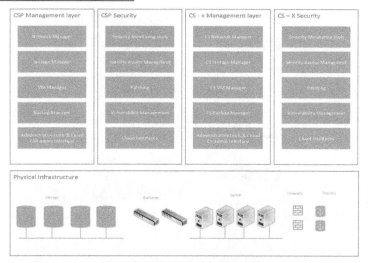

Figure 13 - Public IaaS Cloud Protection scheme

- Public IaaS Cloud Security Infrastructure components can be designed based on isolation concept (See Figure 13, Page 308) and its components are:
  - Isolated CSP Management layer that contains hypervisor, open stack, VM images, CSP backup software, etc.
  - Isolated CSP Security layer that contains security monitoring solutions, Identity access management, etc.
  - CS 1 Isolated Management layer that contains CS management hypervisor, CS backup software, etc.
  - CS 1 Security layer contain security monitoring solutions, Identity access management, etc.
  - Other CS management and security layers.
  - CS IaaS Cloud that is isolated from other tenants IaaS Clouds.

CSP has a management plane contain the (See Figure 13, Page 30) management controls for the entire cloud infrastructure. This management controls control include CSP hypervisor management console, Storage management console, network management, etc. it is isolated through a firewall or one-way gateway. In addition, CSP has another plane that contains Security and monitoring controls such as SIEM, syslog servers, vulnerability management etc. CSs have same two planes managing its part from the cloud. In addition, CS IaaS cloud isolated the part that hosts its production or testing traffic *(Gonzales et al., 2015)*. However, it is important to have visibility on the security posture within the IaaS Cloud, so it is important to design IaaS cloud best protect, isolate sensitive data and to add monitoring controls within inside.

4.1.4 Threat Model

From the author experience, the following points has been observed.

- Cloud Computing attract the same attacker's type that the traditional IT attract and even more.
- CS can receive attacks from other tenants that are sharing the cloud infrastructure with them.
- Cloud Computing brings another threat in addition to the normal threats are there in traditional IT
- VM, Hypervisor, and network manager are a new target that is added a list of targets that are in traditional IT
- Cloud Computing and traditional IT can cause the same damage if security incident happens but the cloud computing has larger threat landscape.

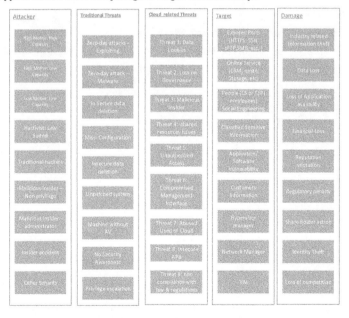

Figure 14 - IaaS Cloud Threat Model

31

Attackers to IaaS infrastructure is more than the attackers that can target traditional datacenter. A CS can be a target from other tenants sharing the resources with him. Besides, the threat landscape is increased because of the nature of the cloud computing technology. In addition, cloud-computing components such as VM hypervisor, network manager, etc. are new targets that CS security administrators monitor & protect them when designing the security strategy.

4.1.5 Governance & Compliance

From the author experience, the following points has been observed.

- Some policies are needed to govern information management in the cloud (See Figure 15, Page 42) such as asset management policy, change management policy, vulnerability management, etc.

- Procedures (e.g. Asset management register, OS patching, OS hardening,) are needed to document how data will be protected by the policies in day to day to day operations.

- International Standard Organization (ISO), National Institute of Standard and Technology (NIST) are organizations that build a standard that governs information in the cloud.

- PC & Laptop, Servers, web-hosting, File hosting, etc are samples of security baselines that garnered the minimum security needed for components that deal with cloud-hosted data.

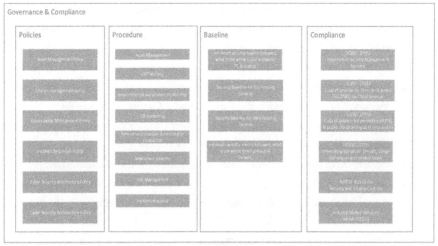

Figure 15 - Governance & Compliance charts in Cloud

Governance ensures that data in cloud information is managed in a secure manner. On top of that monitoring the compliance of security standard that takes care of privacy and security of the information and it will give confidence to CS, CSP, and their customers that the information is protected (See Figure , Page 42).

4.1.6 Controls Used

From the author experience, the following points has been observed.

- Network Security controls: Firewall, IPS, IDS. AD group policy, Software-defined Network, VPN concentrators, WAF. Reverse proxy, Application firewall, Netflow, VLAN, NTP Servers, Syslog, SIEM (See Figure 16, Page 44).

- Hardware & Software secure configuration: Create OS baseline, PC/Server image builder, administration over a secure protocol (SSH, RDP, VNC) or over SSL/IPsec channels, Integrity file checker, Configuration management.

- Controlling of Admin privilege: Enable auditing, least privilege, Password complexity, account creation/access monitoring, multifactor authentication, an Only certain machine that are capable to run administrative tasks, disable service accounts that are not used

- Malware defences: Anti-virus, Network-IPS, Host-IPS, Personal Firewall, Anti-malware - File Reputation, Anti-malware- Sandboxing, DNS Logging.

- Data protection. Risk assessment for sensitive information, Encryption, Database activity monitoring, OS Encryption, Traffic encryption, Application encryption, Need to know controlled access, Audit enabling,
- Asset Management (Hardware/Software): Asset discovery tool, DHCP logging, Network Level Authentication (802.1X), Whitelisting organization application
- Vulnerability Assessment & Remediation: Automatic Vulnerability scanner (Authenticated/unauthenticated mode), Event vulnerability correlations, Patch management, logs monitoring, risk-rating vulnerability.
- Incidents Responses Test custom application through pen-test and auditing
- Email & web browser protection. Harden the systems (remove unnecessary browsers, plugins, mail clients), limit the use of scripts, Proxy (URL Filtering), SPF Filtering, email gateways
- Data Recovery Backup software, Physical security protection for the backup

Network Security
Firewall, IPS, IDS, AD group policy, Software defined Network, VPN concentrators, WAF Reverse proxy, Application firewall, Netflow, VLAN, NTP Servers, Syslog, SIEM

Asset Management (Hardware/Software)
Asset discovery tool, DHCP logging, Network level Authentication (802.1X), White listing organization application

Hardware & Software secure configuration
Create OS baseline, PC/Server image builder administration over secure protocol (SSH, RDP, VNC) or over SSL/IPSEC channels, Integrity file checker, Configuration management

Vulnerability Assessment & Remediation
Automatic Vulnerability scanner (Authenticated/non authenticated mode). Event vulnerability correlations, Patch management, logs monitoring, risk-rating vulnerability

Controlling of Admin privilege
Enable auditing, least privilege. Password complexity, account creation/access monitoring, multifactor authentication. Only certain machine that are capable to run administrator tasks, disable service accounts that are not used

Email & web browser protection
Harden the systems (remove unnecessary browsers, plugins, mail clients) limit the use of scripts, Proxy (URL filtering), SSH Filtering, email gateways

Malware defenses
Anti-virus, Network-IPS, Host-IPS, Personal Firewall, Anti-malware, File Reputation, Anti-malware Sandboxing, DNS Logging

Data Recovery
Backup software, Physical security protection for the backup

Data protections:
Risk assessment for sensitive information, Encryption, Database activity monitoring, OS Encryption, Traffic encryption, Application encryption, Need to know controlled access, Audit enabling.

Incidents Responses
Test custom application through pen-test and auditing

Figure 16 - Controls used for mitigating cloud risk

In general, controls (See Figure , Page 44) can also be classified as a deterrent, preventive corrective, compensative and detective controls (See Figure , Page 44).

36

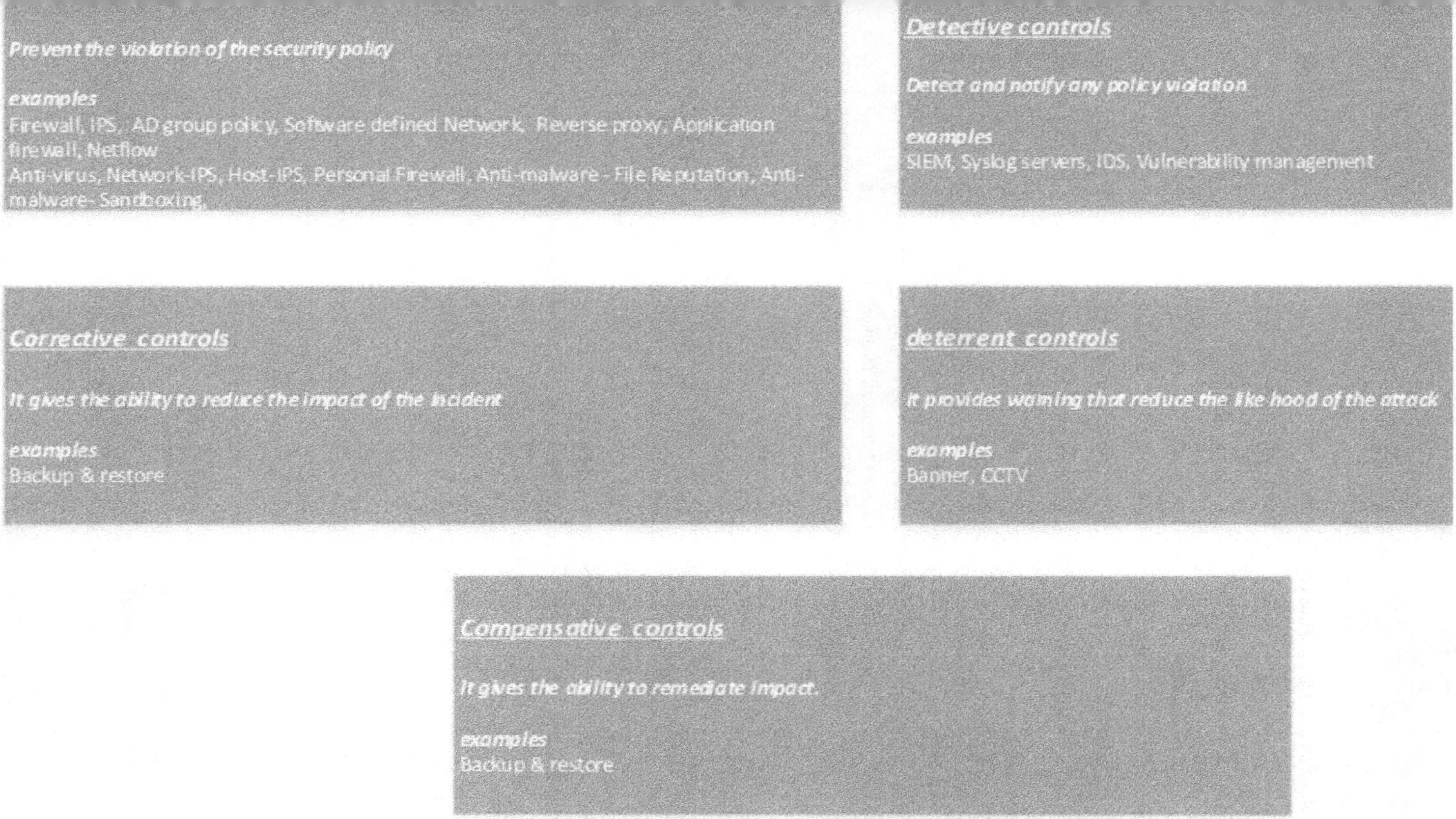

Detective controls

Detect and notify any policy violation

examples
SIEM, Syslog servers, IDS, Vulnerability management

Preventive controls

Prevent the violation of the security policy

examples
Firewall, IPS, AD group policy, Software defined Network, Reverse proxy, Application
Firewall, Netflow
Anti-virus, Network-IPS, Host-IPS, Personal Firewall, Anti-malware - File Reputation, Anti-
malware - Sandboxing

examples
Backup & restore

deterrent controls

It provides warning that reduce the like hood of the attack

examples
Banner, CCTV

Corrective controls

It gives the ability to reduce the impact of the incident

examples
Backup & restore

Compensative controls

It gives the ability to remediate impact.

examples
Backup & restore

Figure 17 - Controls category

A single device can such as a firewall can be a preventive control that can prevent the violation of policy by denying or allow the traffic, and a detective control that can log the traffic passing through it. Besides, a deterrent controls by configuring banner.

The controls used (See Figure , Page 42) should be selected, implemented and monitored based on the risk assessment and business impact analysis. Based on the results of the risk assessment information is classified, controls selected, deployment model, and its placement. The main purpose of the using the security control is to decrease the risk to an acceptable level, which is determined, based on risk assessment.

4.2 Table summary

Item	Observation
Expected growth	• The number of the hyperscale datacenter is expected to be in growth. • Decreasing of Enterprise owned data centres in the next 24 month. • Most of the enterprises tend to utilize the public cloud. • Opportunity for Middle East countries to have attracted hyperscale. datacenters investments. • Attention to cloud security is raised.
Responsibility distributions	• SLA should be developed and monitored to govern the area that CS has no protection on. • CS & CSP has to co-operate to protect IaaS cloud network security. • CS network security should be designed based on isolation (VLANs) to separate sensitive data and user access.
Protection Scheme	• Physical and logical Segregation is mandatory for securing IaaS cloud Infrastructure. • Monitoring should be established isolated inside IaaS cloud (Production servers or testing)
Threat Model	• The threat landscape has been changed from traditional IT • Cloud infrastructure itself became one of the targets
Controls used	• Controls are selected, implemented and monitored based on Risk assessment & business impact analysis. • Information is classified and its location within the cloud is classified.
Governance & compliance	• Following Policies & procedure ensure effective security management process that is in place. • Compliance gives confidence to all parties that information is managed safely.

Table 4 - Observation finding summary

5.0 Chapter 5: Experts Interviews & Data Analysis

5.1 Introduction

The interview method is a very effective way to work with the participants directly to know their complete feedback about the research topic. It is considered a qualitative data collection method that enriches the research with accurate information. In this research, interviews are used to validate the information collected in literature review and observation research methods (See Figure 7, Page 28) as a part of the methodological triangulation validation. The type of the interview is chosen to be semi-structured interviews. Wilson (2012) states that semi-structured gives flexibility for the interviewer that is guided by a set of questions to the researcher on track, then interviewer can follow a topic of interest. Besides, the set of question selected is chosen to be open-ended, which will allow the participants to express and elaborate their point of view with their own words with a complete chance to explain their reasons and answers. Participant is considered an expert in his domain if he has five years or more. Besides, they are selected from different countries in the Middle East. A communication is arranged with them to select a date and time and a location for conducting these interviews. Five information technology experts working in different information technology fields and from different locations (See Table 5, Page 46).

Participant	Country	experience	IT Field
A	Jordan	5	Virtualization (Work with Cloud Consumers)
B	Saudi Arabia	5	Network (Work with Cloud Consumers)
C	Lebanon	6.5	Security/Wireless (Work with Cloud Consumers)
D	Saudi Arabia	16	Security Management (Work with Cloud Consumers)
E	UAE	15	Presales Cloud Computing (Work with Cloud providers)

Table 5- Participants in the interviews

Afterwards, interviews were conducted in the agreed time either it is face to face or it is through telephone due to the availability of the participants, a transcript of these interviews were created and copy was sent to the participants.

5.2 Data Analysis

5.2.1 Expected Growth

All participants were familiar with cloud computing which means that their companies already using its service. Almost all of the interviewees stated that they are using cloud services. For example, engineer H. Bayite, their company are getting IaaS service from Amazon AWS to host a replica of their CRM (Personal Communication, 17 March 2018)

In addition, no one of the interviewees have mentioned that they are using private cloud services except engineer D who has stated that the government are gathering resources to build a very big data center that will host all the ministers IT services as a form of community cloud services (Personal Communication, 18 March 2018). Furthermore, the interviewees state that they have plans for utilizing more cloud services in the next 24 months and in return, their organizations will be less dependent on their own data centre. According to engineer H. Bayite, they are planning not to have any physical server in the future and host all of their infrastructures in Amazon AWS cloud (Personal Communication, 17 March 2018)

5.2.2 Responsibility distribution and protection scheme

Normally, the clouds service provider has complete responsibility for the physical security of the data centre by putting design all applicable controls to secure it such as CCTV, fences, fire control systems. However, engineer B states that his organization is putting their racks in cages, secure it with a lock, and keep all its keys (Personal communication, 14 March 2018). All interviewees that work with cloud consumers (See Table 5, Page 39) state that they are taking care of the security of the operating systems by doing patching and implementing a firewall, IPS, updating antiviruses and take care of data security and privacy. Nevertheless, engineer E which work with a service provider states that they can offer patching service as a part of a package. Besides, he states that service level of agreement (SLA) will grantee the level of service consumer can get, document the responsibility and escalations. (Personal communication, 26 March 2018). In addition, Engineer A stated as they are providing some cloud services that they will only be responsible for physical and the networking layer or servers underlying layers (Personal communication, 12 March 2018). Besides, engineer C, states that they are using their provider to patch their systems and Antivirus (Personal communication, 17 March 2018). Therefore, SLA is a contract that will identify the responsibility of each party, how it will be done and monitor. The responsibility is different from consumer to another based on the SLA. In addition, According to C, consumers use firewalls and IPS to ensuring isolation between them and rest of the public cloud consumer's neighbours (Personal communication, 17 March 2018).

5.2.3 Threat Landscape, Practices and Controls used

All the interviewees are agreeing that availability, infrastructure readiness is one of the key benefits of utilizing cloud services that this will offload the headache of preserving traditional IT availability. In traditional IT, the datacenter's engineers protect the server farms from inside users and external user. H. Bayite mentioned that internal threats can be eliminated or reduced by adopting infrastructure (Personal communication, 17 March 2018). However, engineer E new threats have been added to the threat landscape due to cloud computing nature such as sharing resources among different consumers and threats from another neighboring cloud consumer (Personal communication, 18 March 2018).

With almost same practice and controls that are being used in traditional IT such as AV, patching, next-generation firewalls, IPS, Data encryption, DNS securities, Cloud consumers are protecting their cloud infrastructure networks and sensitive data. Engineer E who works at a cloud service provider state that a secure channel for the consumer to access their data, encryption for data in the storage, strong authentication and strong service level of agreement are essential for could security (Personal communication, 26 March 2018). In addition, engineer D mentioned that they are following ISO standard and best practice in configuring, operating and monitoring security control for protecting their cloud infrastructure. Besides, they follow up with periodic audits to comply with the standard which achieves acceptable way for managing their data in the cloud securely (Personal communication, 26 March 2018).

5.2.4 Governance and compliance

Policy and procedures play very important roles in ensuring that information is managed securely in cloud or on-premises. Most of the interviewees agreed about the importance of policies and procedures in dealing with the information and its security. Besides, it should be different as the threat landscape is different in cloud computing. Many threats have been introduced and some other has been reduced. Engineer D states that the policies and procedures should be more specific and in more details to address who will access the data in all its life cycle and how (Personal communications, 18 March 2018).

In addition, Certificate and compliance give cloud consumer's confidence for utilizing cloud computing services. Engineer B elaborate on this confidence and said it means more security measures in cheaper price (Personal communications, 14 March 2018). In addition, compliance enables monitoring the whole process from a third party. Engineer D, mentioned that compliance permits a third party to check the effectiveness of the policies, procedures and controls.

5.3 Table summary

Item	Interview's collected information
Expected growth	• All interviewees are interested in cloud computing. • The government are going to build a hyperscale data centre for their ministries. • All interviewees companies have planned for utilizing more cloud adoption • An Interviewee mentioned that his company will not use any more hardware on-premises. Instead, they will utilize the cloud. • Utilizing cloud services will make companies less dependent on enterprise-owned data centre
Responsibility	• SLA draft the responsibility between the CSP and CS agreement between the two parties. • Some interviewees co-operate with the CSP to protect the network security and sometimes physical security. • Isolation is done by using firewalls in the cloud.
Protection Scheme	• Using a firewall for isolations bring by necessity VLAN segregation. • Monitoring controls logs to make sure that IaaS is secure
Threat Model	• Cloud computing eliminates the threat of service disruption by high availability of cloud design. • Hosting services to cloud eliminate company inside threats and focus on external threats • New threats have been raised due to the nature of cloud computing (e.g. sharing the resources).
Controls used	• ISO 27002:2013 and best practice in configuring, operating and monitoring security control for protecting their cloud infrastructure. • Encryption for data in the storage, strong authentication and strong service level of the agreement is essential for could security. • Firewalls, IPS, anti-malware.
Governance and	• All interviewees agreed on the importance of policies and

compliance	procedures.
	• More Compliance and certificates mean better security measure.
	• Compliance permits a third party to check the effectiveness of the policies, procedures and controls.

Table 6 - Interview's collected data

5.4 triangular validation and confirmation

The purpose of using this method is to compare information collected in the literature review and observation research methods (See Table 4, Page 385) with the information collecting during the interviewees for validation and confirmations. Besides, it will enrich and strengthens the researcher's information (Bekhet & Zauszniewski, 2012). The expected growth is confirmed as per as the interview results. In addition, this confirmed expected growth for cloud usage in the future create a demand for a strategy or a framework that will organize cloud security efforts. This growth should be governed by a complete understanding of the cloud associated risks that will help government and organizations in the region to have the cloud benefits safely. With well-written service level of agreement, most of the consumers are willing to protect themselves when using cloud services and monitor the sharing of the responsibilities as per as observations & interview data collection results. In addition, the threat landscape is changing when utilizing more cloud computing services. Nevertheless, there is no well formal framework or strategy they are using that organize cloud-computing security. Instead, some of them are complying in an ad-hoc basis. They are doing the same controls that are used in traditional IT and just extending these controls in the cloud without a strategy except for using ISO 27002:2013 code of practice for information security controls that are not specialized for cloud computing, but it is for information security in general. Some of the interviewees like engineer C indicate is that the policies are almost the same which gives us impressaion that not all the organization are familiar with all the risks associated with cloud adoption. For examples, not all of the interviewees mentioned anything about risks that associated with cloud adoption like vendor lock-in, CSP malicious insider, management interface compromise, etc, that reflects that there is no clarity about what resides in the cloud. However, most of the intreviewees agreed on that the policies need to be modified to address the changes in threat landscape in cloud computing. Finally, the cloud computing intreducing new benefits and the other hand new threats. Middle East countries need a templete to be used that cover most of the concerns in cloud computing technology. Using this templete should be clear, eazy and compensiate possible lack of secuirty experience from either the provider or from the consumers.

6.0 chapter 6: Discussions

After reviewing knowledge feedbacks from information technology's experts interviews, there is a need for a template to help cloud practitioner to in cloud adoption. However, each organization has its own risk profile, which varies depending on the company nature. Besides, depending on the risk apatite or risk tolerance of the organizations, acceptable level of risk is identified as it governs all the information security activities (ISACA, 2011). Therefore, the type of data hosted in the cloud will be identified based on this acceptable risk. In this research, Cloud seekers will be divided to a conservative where the acceptable risk level is slow and companies that have high-risk tolerance where the acceptable risk level is high, so each type of organizations would require different template that will identify what is the data to be adopted, how to design and to protect. This template will be designed based on isolation of trust zones. Gonzales et al (2015) state the cloud security model is based on the isolation between tenants cloud IaaS traffic, CSP cloud management (e.g. VM manager (hypervisor), network manager, storage manager, VM images), CSP cloud security monitoring traffic, CS cloud management and CS cloud security monitoring traffic (See Figure 4, Page 22). Firewalls are the key player in the isolation between different networks which have the main concept to prevent unauthorized access through implementation of access controls (ACL) (Zhang, 2014). For enforcing comprehensive access control, robust identity and access management systems (IAM) are needed. Gonzales et al (2015) state that these IAM systems may use active directory and multi-factor authentications with time-limited access code that enables. Active directory enables centralized management, security controlling of network computer accounts and encrypting data sent to the destinations to the source (Melber, 2004). Domain controllers can be read-only domain controllers (RODC) that can provide security feature that can be used in untrusted network zone, for example, unidirectional replication that prevent malicious updates or changes to be done from it but only receive the changes from reading and write domain controllers that are located in more trusted zones, besides, it does not allow password to be cached which means that passwords can not be obtained in case of it get compromised (Microsoft, 2012). Gonzales et al (2015) state cloud service provider trust zone (CSP TZ) contains components that manage the cloud infrastructure (See Table 8, Page 46) cloud tenants IAM servers and CSP information system security (CSP IS3). In general, IS3 (See Table 7, Page 45) gives CSP or CS full visibility and track of every activity, vulnerability, and event.

Security Controls	Description	Compliance Standard
Security Information and Event Monitoring (SIEM)	it collects, correlates and analyses logs generated from network and security nodes, operating systems and applications, besides, it generates reports that have full visibility on the organization security posture (Stephenson, 2014)	NIST 800-53 IR - 5
Vulnerability Management software	it scans the nodes for detecting missing patches, vulnerabilities or misconfigured settings and software (Kovács, et al., 2013), in general, it is consists of manager and scanner	NIST 800-53 RA - 5
Netflow Analyzer	it provides full visibility for all traffic that crosses the network node (e.g. Firewall) (Santos, 2015)	NIST 800-53 SI - 4
Asset Management software	Its main purpose to discover and have an inventory of all components of the organization's information systems within the authorized boundary (NIST, 2018a).	NIST 800-53 CM - 8
Identity Access Management Software (e.g. DC, RODC, etc.)	Active directory can be used to authenticate, authorize and account users and computer account (Melber, 2004).	NIST 800-53 IA - 2
Syslog Servers	It captures logs for analysis for previous period of time (Liu, 2009)	NIST 800-53 AU - 12
Reverse proxy servers/Anti-malware/ proxy servers	it helps in protection from malicious code that can be executed locally or from a remote place and have a direct impact on confidentiality, integrity and security (NIST, 2018b)	NIST 800-53 SI-3

Table 7 - IS3 controls

Besides, it will help to identify which event is an incident that could have an impact on availability, confidentiality and integrity, Furthermore; it gives the option for incident response (Wenge, et al., 2014). The controls selected (See Table 7, Page 45) are based on the NIST 800-53 as it is the best practices that became indeed the main standard and guideline for security and privacy controls for the private sector and government it is freely available (NIST, 2013).

Security Controls	Description
ESXi	Provides bare-metal virtualization of servers so you can consolidate your applications on less hardware.
vCenter Server	Provides a centralized platform for managing vSphere environments.
vCenter Site Recovery Manager	Provides disaster recovery capability that lets you perform automated orchestration and no disruptive testing for virtualized applications.
vRealize Automation	Provides functionality for deploying and provisioning of business-relevant cloud services across private and public clouds, physical infrastructure, hypervisors, and public cloud providers.
vRealize Automation Application Services	Provides automated application provisioning in the cloud including deploying and configuring the application's components and dependent middleware platform services on infrastructure clouds.
vRealize Business for vSphere	Provides transparency and control over the costs and quality of IT services that are critical for private or hybrid cloud success.
vRealize Configuration Manager	Provides automation of configuration and compliance management across your virtual, physical and cloud environments, assessing them for operational and security compliance.
vRealize Hyperic	Provides monitoring of operating systems, middleware and applications running in physical, virtual, and cloud environments.
vRealize Infrastructure Navigator	Provides automated discovery of application services, visualizes relationships, and maps dependencies of applications on virtualized compute, storage and network resources.
vRealize Orchestrator	Provides the capability to create workflows that automate activities such as provisioning a virtual machine, performing scheduled maintenance, initiating backups, and many others.
vRealize Operations Manager	Provides comprehensive visibility and insights into the performance, capacity and health of your infrastructure.
vSphere Big Data Extensions	Simplifies running Big Data workloads on the vSphere platform.
vSphere Data Protection	Provides advanced data protection with backup and recovery to disk.
vSphere Replication	Provides replication, at the individual virtual machine disk level, between data stores hosted on any storage.

Table 8 - CSP cloud management zone components (VMware, 2018)

However, identity access management depends on proper data classifications because based on this data classification authentication and authorization is implemented, furthermore, before adoption data must be classified based (See Table 9, Page 47) on classification terminology (Simorjay, 2014).

Sensitivity	Terminology model 1	Terminology model 2
High	Confidential	Restricted
Medium	For internal use only	Sensitive
Low	Public	Unrestricted

Table 9 - Data classification Severities and terminologies *(Simorjay, 2014, p. 7)*

Organizations must identify the level of sensitivity that is suitable for their risk appetite. Nevertheless, the suggested template is build depending on the fact that not all companies or organization has the same risk appetite. Therefore, templates should be customizable based on the risk that the organization faced. For this purpose, two different templates will be discussed.

- Low-risk tolerant companies.
- High-risk tolerant companies.

Deployment model	Disadvantage	Description
Public	Lack of control	The data is not in the consumer premises custody, instead, it is managed by the third party
	Slow Speed	The service is provided over the internet
	Resources Shared	The resources are shared from
Private	Capacity Ceiling	Due to the physical limitation of the hardware
	Higher cost	it is higher from public cloud

Table 10 - Cloud deployment model disadvantage (Srilakshmi, et al., 2013)

Finally, adopting data in public cloud is associated (See Table 10, Page 47) with more risk than public cloud. Therefore, it will not be suitable for adapting data high sensitive data (See Table 9, Page 47).

6.1 Low-risk appetite template.

Here, Low-risk means that the level of risk that the organization can take is very low, and this is might be because they are risk cautious and circumspect as they are concentrating on stable profit and growth. Besides, they might be concentrating on avoid market fluctuations, and this is driven by the influence of regulations, laws, competitions, profit margin, culture, etc. (RIMS, 2012). The new template is trying to map data, services and protection controls for a different kind of IaaS cloud deployment model. For example, high severity data (e.g. trade secrets, medical records, customer information, employees' information, etc.) are suggested to be adopted in private cloud deployment model (See Table 11, Page 48), however, lower sensitive information are suggested to be adopted for community and public cloud deployment model.

Data sensitivity	Example	Deployment model
High	Medical records, customer information, trade secrets, trade secrets.	Private
Medium/High	Shared information due to regulations (e.g. some medical records that are shared between hospitals and government)	Community
Medium/Low	UAT environments, developing environments	Public

Table 11 - Suggested type of data for different deployment models in low risk template

Due to the higher risk associated with the IaaS cloud infrastructure, cloud arch 4 (See *Table 2*, Page 21) are suggested to be used in public cloud. Gonzales et al (2015) state Arch 4 has cloud infrastructure cloud hardening measure by which VM files is secured at rest by encryption, VM files in motion (VM migration) are encrypted, and CS and CSP IAM servers are configured to give limited access for CSP or CS engineers with 2 factors authentication with time limited code. NIST has introduced a functionality to give the server to verify the authenticity of the CPU when booting (Regenscheid, 2012 cited in Gonzales et al, 2015). Furthermore, application whitelisting is configured for server, which prevent unauthorized application for installing it.

In this template (See Figure 18, Page 58), the user acceptance testing and development environment are suggested to be developed in public cloud, while the private cloud have all application front end, databases, cloud managements, and Security monitoring Zones.

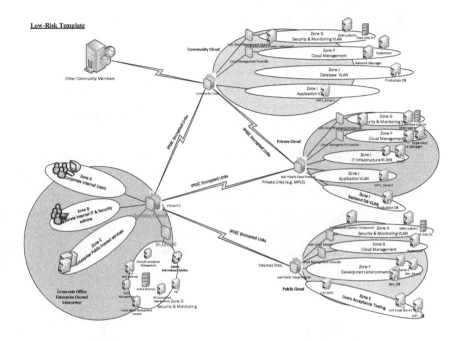

Figure 18 – Suggested Low risk cloud security infrastructure template.

Internet links is connecting remote users through VPN concentrators in corporate Office to have the same security measures for the internal users. Besides, customers can reach company applications hosted in cloud through internet links connected to private cloud infrastructure. There is only one read and write domain controllers that are hosted in corporate main office, rest domain controllers are read-only domain controllers.

6.2 High-risk appetite template.

Here, high-risk means that the level of risk that the organization can take is high, and this is might be because their risk appitite are high as the level of accepting losses increase as they seeks higher profits and gains, this might be due to absense of reputatuions, increaseing of the competions and high profit margin (RIMS, 2012). Utilizing public cloud services will give cloud consumers IT services with lower cost as a direct benefit (Haeberlen and Dupre, 2012).

Data sensitivity	Example	Deployment model
High/Medium/Low	Most of the companies data	Private
Medium/High	Shared information due to regulations (e.g. some medical records that are shared between hospitals and government)	Community

Table 12 - Suggested type of data for different deployment models in High risk template

In this template (See Figure 19, page 6), data will be distributed between enterprise office servers and public cloud. To ensure security also, it is suggested to use Arch 4 when hardening IaaS public cloud infrastructure (See *Table 2*, Page 21). All security solution are centrally managed from a main office location such as centralized management for the firewall, centralize vulnerability management solution, etc. In addition, continuous audit and monitoring of the security posture of public cloud is mandatory (Gonzales et al., 2015).

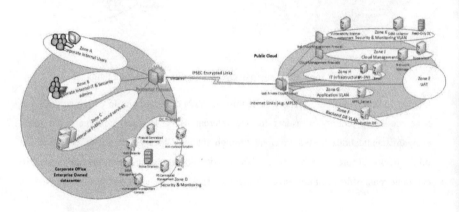

Figure 19 – High-risk appetite template

Chapter 7: Data Collection & Analysis

7.1 Introduction

The purpose of having conducted a survey is to validate the results from Phase 1 of the research (See Figure 7, Page 28) with the information collected from literature review and discussions. It creates a second stage of methodological triangulation validation. Besides, research finding will be strengthened by critic review of the IT professionals (Denzin, 1978 citied in Bekhet & Zauszniewski, 2012). Furthermore, it will link the research with the market to see does the research answer market needs and help enhance the security in the region or not. The survey will be based on a closed-ended question by which answers are predefined that would seek candidate feedback over the template created and one open-ended question that will give the candidate more margin to speaks about the research finding.

The survey consists of 13 closed-ended question discussing feedback regarding the template that was discussed in details the last chapter and one open-ended question that will make the candidate have more margin to speak about the templates. The survey will be conducted electrically using Google Form and distributed by social media (e.g. LinkedIn and Gmail). Electronic surveys are very simple in administration, distribution and low cost (Magero et al, 2015). The survey can be accessed through Google form[3]. The survey population are basically the same experts who did the interviews, besides, it will be publish through author page on LinkedIn to widen the range of the population for better and accurate results. The survey consists of three main section. Firstly, address the cloud security weaknesses in the market. Secondly, feedback regarding the low-risk appetite template. Finally, feedback high-risk appetite template. Besides, open-end question that will measure the effectiveness of the research.

7.2 Data Analysis

All of the responses comes with negative feedback about the visibility of the security posture for data in the cloud. The respondent (See Figure 20, Page 62) either have concerns or do not have any visibility over the security of their data in the cloud. Besides, all of them see that the expertise for cloud security professionals cannot be found easily. Furthermore, all of the respondents agree that existence of a guiding template will help them in cloud security

---

3 https://docs.google.com/forms/d/e/1FAIpQL9Sflya3d-
atUMc9a5RCkis8l9rhNtaKrwvLbjhfTk5TZ9MTugA/viewform

adoption. This answers expressing that the results of this research address market demand and it will help IT professionals in the region solving their problems.

Do you think that you have full visibility for the security posture for your data in cloud and risks associated with it?

6 responses

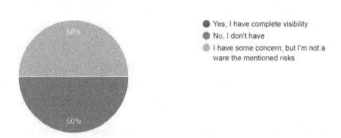

- Yes, I have complete visibility
- No, I don't have
- I have some concern, but I'm not a ware the mentioned risks

Figure 20 – Professionals' visibility over data security and risks in the cloud.

The second section of the survey discuss key information related to the low-risk appetite template. Firstly, Over 80 (See Figure 21, Page 63) percent of the respondent agrees that isolation between zones is achieve via this template through using firewalls and VLANs. Firewalls isolate CSP Management, CS Management, CS Security & monitoring, CS IaaS in good architecture, etc. In addition, almost 16% does not agree that the controls mentioned in the template (See Table 7, Page 45) will achieve visibility of the security posture in cloud. Besides, half of the candidates agrees that Cloud management zone components (See Table 8, Page 46) establish control over the IaaS infrastructure, while the rest of the candidate is not fully sure but they did not disagree. In addition, almost 66% of candidates agree that cloud management zone (See Table 2, Page 21) is hardened by using Arch 4. Finally, the majority of the candidates are agreeing that the data classification distribution (See Table 11, Page 48) across different deployment model is effective.

Do you think that Isolation is achieved in this template?

6 responses

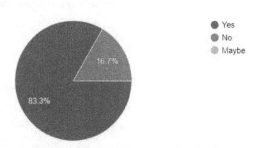

Figure 21 – Candidates feedback regarding isolation of zones in low-risk appetite template

For the high-risk appetite template, almost 66% of the candidate agreed about the achievement of the isolation via VLANs and firewall. About the visibility of security posture (See Figure 22, Page 64), less than 17% of the candidates are not confident of the security posture of their data in the cloud. For the data distribution (See *Table 12*, Page 50), 66% of the candidates agree that the severity distribution across different cloud deployment is effective. However, the majority of candidates agrees that the management controls (See *Table 8*, Page 46) are the same between the two mentioned templates.

Do you think the below controls are enough to have full visibility on the security posture in Public cloud?

6 responses

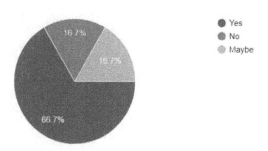

Figure 22 – candidates respond about the visibility on their security posture in public cloud

Furthermore, for both templates the majority of the candidates agrees that following these templates will help in securing their data in cloud, but it should be enforced with comprehensive incident response plan that is handled by good trained experienced engineers, implementing of intrusion prevention systems that enforce the infrastructure with threat intelligence and establishment of security awareness program for the staff.

Finally, all the results were strengthen the value of this research as it confirm the research results about the need of a template that will guide and help the engineers in the reigion for the data cloud adoption, which will compensate the lack of coud security exertise. In addition, it will give full visiability for the business about the opportuity in cloud especially for start up companies and small to medium business that they don't have the finnaical resources for investing in security products. Furethermore, it will guide engineers for the selection of the type of data suitable for each cloud deployments (e.g. (See Table 11, Page 48), (See *Table 12*, Page 50), etc). Therfore, IT proffisional must run a risk assessent (See Figure 2, Page 21) to identify what information they own that have high, medium and low sensitivity for their business (Haeberlen and Dupre, 2012). Then, accourding to their companies risk apetite the tamplate type and the deployment models is selected.

Chapter 8: Summary

8.1 Summary

Cloud computing is a new model of Information technology that enables on-demand self-managed IT services access to shared pool of resources such as characteristics of broad network access, rapid elasticity, resources pooling, and on-demand access. In addition, despite the dynamic nature of the cloud utilization for any consumer, the utilized resources are monitored, metered, controlled and reported through an agreement called service level of agreement (SLA). In chapter 2, a literature review was conducted to explore the latest research finding and the following information was concluded. Cloud computing decreases the amount of start-up investment for a business that will enable reducing the starting cost and only to pay what is a consumer is utilizing which is very important to stimulate investment in the Middle East. Besides, cloud service providers (CSPs) are a large scale investor who can afford to invest in security in terms of hiring the required expertise and implementing the most recent advanced security technology to provide them to their consumers by relatively smaller investments as the cost will be distributed among all the cloud consumers (CS). Nevertheless, there are risks associated with cloud adoption which were not there before in traditional IT such as data lock-in, loss of governance, malicious CSP insiders, insecure data deletion, issues related to shared resources, management interface compromises, etc. In addition, the designing of the cloud security infrastructure based on the isolation concept between different zones of the IaaS (e.g. CSP cloud management zone, CSP security and monitoring zone, CSs IaaS cloud traffic, CS cloud management zone, CS security and monitoring zone).

In chapter 4, observation research methods were explored, and the following are some conclusions that were drawn. In middle east countries, there are more challenges facing the cloud adoption such as lack of security expertise for cloud security, lack of confidence in the security of their data in the cloud, and lack of formalised strategy that guide cloud consumers for safely cloud adoption processes. Nevertheless, there is a potential for growth in this sector in the region. There are expected huge growth in the organization that are using leaving enterprise owned data center and IaaS (See Table 4, Page 38).

In chapter 5, Experts interviews were explored mainly to verify the information collected form observation research and literature review method. The following information where validated. Because of lack of cloud's security expertise and the expected growth for the IaaS cloud services in the region, IaaS cloud adoption process is ad-hoc bases. Therefore, there is a need for a template that will guide the IT professionals in cloud data adoption process despite of the technical cloud security background of the IT professionals.

In this research (chapter 6), a solution for all of this issues was discussed. Organizations will have a template to be followed to guide them through their cloud adoption process. This template contains the utilization of different kind of IaaS deplouyment model that are integrated togther. It will be followed for guiding organizations in designing their entire IaaS security infrastructure based, data selection for each IaaS cloud deployment model, and the controls used for establishing governance and control over the cloud infrastructure. It starts with a risk assessment for organization IT infrastructure to identify the sensitivity of information and organization's risk appetite. Based on risk appetite, the organization's IT professionals will choose which template to follow. For example, low-risk appetite organizations that are very conservative and their acceptable risk is very low will follow Low-risk appetite (See Section 6.1, Page 48). However, high-risk appetite organizations that can accept the higher acceptable risk will follow high-risk appetite template (See Section 6.2, Page 49). Afterwards, Organizations will have full visibility about data placement in the cloud realm, cloud security infrastructure design, cloud management controls that are responsible to establish a degree of governance in the cloud, security and monitoring controls that will be in line with NIST standards to have full visibility on the cloud security posture, and it will guide organization in SLA negotiation. Furthermore, these templates can be used either by cloud service provider (CSP) or the cloud consumer (CS) for designing the cloud security infrastructure.

In chapter 7, survey is conducted and its findings were explored. Its main purpose is to validate the findings that was explored in chapter 6. The participants that were from different IT background and they expressed the importance of the existence of these kind of templates to encourage them for safely utilizing IaaS services.

8.2 Conclusion

Finally, cloud computing has a room for growth in the Middle East countries. This research is discovering the needs for faciltating IaaS cloud utilization safely. IT professionals will follow these no need of deep understanding of IaaS security concerns. The templates are developed bases on ENISA and NIST recommendation. Besides, different controls used are in line of NIST SP 800-53 standard that focuses on Security and Privacy Controls. For using these templates, IT professionals must identify their data sensitivity and their risk appetite. Then they will have all the required information that will guide them in negotiation of SLA in terms of designing the isolation, CSP roles and responsibility and CS roles and responsibilities.

8.3 Recommendations

To take benefits of the room for growth and the strategic location of the Middle East countries as they are located in the middle of the way between east and west (See Figure 11, Page 36). Therefore, these countries especially Egypt are nominated to host investment of implementing hyper-scale data centres as it will be located relatively near to host cloud computing processing.

In addition, there is a need to enhance the security of the template discussed in this research by conducting research in enhancements in identity access management (IAM), monitoring the security posture of the IaaS environment, data privacy in IaaS cloud, anti-malware techniques.

References

Alali, F. A. and Yeh, C.-L. (2012) "Cloud Computing: Overview and Risk Analysis," Journal of Information Systems [Online], 26 (2), pp. 13–33.

Alassafi, M. O. et al. (2017) "A framework for critical security factors that influence the decision of cloud adoption by Saudi government agencies," Telematics and Informatics,[Online], 34(7), pp. 996–1010

ARMBRUST, M. et al., 2010. A view of cloud computing. communications of the ACM,[Online], 53(4), pp. 51-58

Baker, L. M., 2006. Observation: a complex research method. Library Trends, [Online], 55(1), pp171+.

Barnett, T., Sumits, A., Jain , S. & Khurana , T., 2016. Cisco Global Cloud Index 2015-2020. [Online] Available at: https://www.cisco.com/c/dam/m/en_us/service-provider/ciscoknowledgenetwork/files/622_11_15-16-Cisco_GCI_CKN_2015-2020_AMER_EMEAR_NOV2016.pdf [Accessed 3 December 2017].

Beck , S. E. & Manuel, K., 2008. Practical research methods for librarians and information professionals. [Online], New York: Neal-Schuman.

Bekhet, A. & Zauszniewski, J. A., 2012. Methodological Triangulation: An Approach to Understanding Data. Nurse Researcher, 20(2), pp. 40-43

Blokland, K., Mengerink, J. & Pol, M., 2013. Testing Cloud Services. [Online], Santa Barbara, CA: Rooky Nook.

Cisco, 2015. Cisco Global Cloud Index. [Online], available at http://www.cisco.com/en/US/solutions/collateral/ns341/ns525/ns537/ns705/ns1175/Cloud_Index_White_Paper.html#wp9000816 [Accessed 3 December 2017].

Cloud Security Alliance, 2017a. Custom Applications and IaaS Trends 2017, [Online], US:Cloud Security Alliance, Available at: https://downloads.cloudsecurityalliance.org/assets/survey/custom-applications-and-iaas-trends-2017.pdf [Accessed 8 November 2016].

Cloud Security Alliance, 2017b. Software Defined Perimeter for Infrastructure as a Service, [Online], US:Cloud Security Alliance, Available at: https://downloads.cloudsecurityalliance.org/assets/research/sdp/sdp_for_iaas.pdf [Accessed 8 November 2016].

Gaurav, S. and Shuchi (2016) "Cloud Computing and its Adoption Challenges," International Research Journal of Engineering and Technology, [Online], 3(4), pp. 2648–2654

Gonzales, D. Kaplan, J. Saltzman, E. Winkelman, Z., & Woods, D. (2015) "Cloud-Trust - a Security Assessment Model for Infrastructure as a Service (IaaS) Clouds," IEEE Transactions on Cloud Computing,[Online], 5(3) p523-536.

Gordon, 2015. The Official (ISC)2 Guide to the CCSP CBK. 2 ed.[Online], Indianapolis, IN: John Wiley & Sons, Inc..

Groves, R. et al., 2009. Survey Methodology. 2nd ed. [Online], Hoboken.: John Wiley & Sons

Haeberlen, T. & Dupré, L, 2012. Cloud computing benefits risks and recommendations for information security, [Online] EU: European Union Agency for Network and Information Security (ENISA), Available at: https://resilience.enisa.europa.eu/cloud-security-and-resilience/publications/cloud-computing-benefits-risks-and-recommendations-for-information-security [Accessed 8 November 2016].

Hausman, K., Cook, L., & Sampaio, T., 2013. Cloud Essentials: CompTIA Authorized Courseware for Exam CLO-001 (1), [Online] Somerset, US: Sybex. ProQuest ebrary. [Assessed at 7 December 2016].

He, X., Chomsiri, T., Nanda, P. & Tan, Z., 2014. Improving Cloud network security. Future Generation Computer Systems, [Online], 30(1), pp. 116-126.

Iorga, M. & Karmel, A., 2015. Managing Risk in Cloud Echosystem. [Online] Available at: http://ws680.nist.gov/publication/get_pdf.cfm?pub_id=919234 [Accessed 1 December 2015].

ISACA (2011) CISM Review Manual 2012. 13th ed. Edited by M. Broadly. [Online], Illinois, United States of America: ISACA.

Kovács, L., Kozlovszky, M., Törőcsik, M., Windisch, G., Ács, S., Prém, D., Eigner, G., Sas, P., 2013. Cloud security monitoring and vulnerability. IEEE 17th International Conference on Intelligent Engineering Systems, [Online], 1(1), pp. 265 - 269

Krutz, R. L. and Vines, R. D. (2010) Cloud security : a comprehensive guide to secure cloud computing. [Online], Indianapolis, Ind: Wiley.

LaGesse, D. (2009) "taking a walk to cloud": U.S News & World Report, [Online], 146 (2), pp. 71–74

Liu, D., 2009. Cisco Router and Switch Forensics. Burlington, MA: Syngress Publishing, Inc..

Melber, D., 2004. Windows Active Directory Group Policy Objects.. Internal Auditing,[Online], 19(4), pp. 38-42.

Magro, M. J., Prybutok, V. R. & Rayan, S. D., 2015. How survey administration can affect response in the electronic surveys. Quality and Quantity, [Online], 49(5), p. 2145–2154.

Mell, P. & Grance, T., 2011. The NIST definition of cloud computing (NIST SP 800-145), [Online], Gaithersburg: U.S. Department of Commerce, Available at: http://nvlpubs.nist.gov/nistpubs/Legacy/SP/nistspecialpublication800-145.pdf [Accessed 16 June 2017].

Microsoft, 2012. Advantages That an RODC Can Provide to an Existing Deployment. [Online] Available at: https://docs.microsoft.com/en-us/previous-versions/windows/it-pro/windows-server-2008-R2-and-2008/cc770320(v=ws.10)

Microsoft, 2018. Shared Responsibilities for Cloud Computing. [Online] Available at: https://gallery.technet.microsoft.com/Shared-Responsibilities-81d0ff91 [Accessed 3 March 2018].

Mint, 2016. Future of cloud computing. [Online] New Delhi: ProQuest, Available at: http://search.proquest.com/docview/1814016300/abstract/715410F05042457FPQ/1?a ccountid=8318 [Accessed 2 December 2017].

NIST Roadmap Working group, 2013. NIST Cloud Computing Standards Roadmap. [Online] Available at: http://nvlpubs.nist.gov/nistpubs/SpecialPublications/NIST.SP.500-291r2.pdf

NIST, 2018a. NIST Special Publication 800-53 (Rev. 4). [Online] Available at: https://nvd.nist.gov/800-53/Rev4/control/CM-8

NIST, 2018b. NIST Special Publication 800-53 (Rev. 4). [Online] Available at: https://nvd.nist.gov/800-53/Rev4/control/SI-3

Obasuyi, G. and Sari, A. (2015) "Security Challenges of Virtualization Hypervisors in Virtualized Hardware Environment," Journal of Communications, Network and System, [Online], 8(July), pp. 260–273

RIMS, 2012. Exploring Risk Appetite and Risk Tolerance,[Online], New York, NY: RIMS.

Robinson, N. et al. (2011) "Understanding the implications for security, privacy and trust," in The Cloud. RAND Corporation., pp. 22–27. Available at: https://www.jstor.org/stable/pdf/10.7249/tr933ec.8.pdf. [Accessed 1 December 2017]

Ruboczki, E. S. and Rajnai, Z. (2015) "Moving towards Cloud Security," Interdisciplinary Description of Complex Systems, [Online], 13(1), pp. 9–14.

Santos, O., 2015. Network Security with NetFlow and IPFIX: Big Data Analytics for Information Security. Indianapolis, Indiana : Cisco Press.

Simorjay, F., 2014. Data classification for cloud readiness. [Online] Available at: https://download.microsoft.com/download/0/A/3/0A3BE969-85C5-4DD2-83B6-366AA71D1FE3/Data-Classification-for-Cloud-Readiness.pdf [Accessed 27 April 2018].Suleman, M. (2016) Cyber Security in the Middle East. [Online], Available at: https://www.infosecurity-magazine.com/blogs/cyber-security-in-the-middle-east/ [Accessed 3 December 2017].

Stephenson, P. 2014, "SIEM", SC Magazine, [Online],vol. 25, no. 4, pp. 36.

Srilakshmi, M., Veenadhari, C. & Pradeep, I., 2013. Deployment models of Cloud Computing: Challenge. International Journal of Advanced Research in Computer Science, [Online], 4(9), pp. 135-138

Vaquero, L. M., Rodero-Merino, L. & Moran, D., 2011. Locking the sky: a survey on IaaS cloud Security. Springer-Verlag, [Online],91(1), pp. 93-118.

VMware (2011) "Business Agility and the True Economics of Cloud Computing," VMware. [Online], Available at: https://www.vmware.com/files/pdf/accelerate/VMware_Business_Agility_and_the_True_Economics_of_Cloud_Computing_White_Paper.pdf. [Accessed 3 December 2017].

VMware, 2018. Introduction to vCloud Suite. [Online] Available at: http://pubs.vmware.com/vcloudsuite-60/index.jsp?topic=%2Fcom.vmware.vcloudsuite.doc%2FGUID-0E5C898E-BF9C-4079-A755-DD8570EC3C97.html [Accessed 25 April 2018].

Wenge, O., Lampe, U., Rensing, C. & Steinmetz, R., 2014. Security Information and Event Monitoring as a Service: a Survey on Current Concerns and Solutions. DE GRUYTER, 37(2), pp. 163-170.

Wilson, V., 2012. Research Methods: Interviews. Evidence Based Library and Information Practice,[Online], 7(2), pp. 96-98.

Zhang, W., 2014. DESIGN OF FIREWALL SECURITY CONTROL PROGRAM. Applied Mechanics and Materials,[Online], Volume 556-562, pp. 5999-6002.

Appendix 1 – Research Work Flow

Dissertation workflow

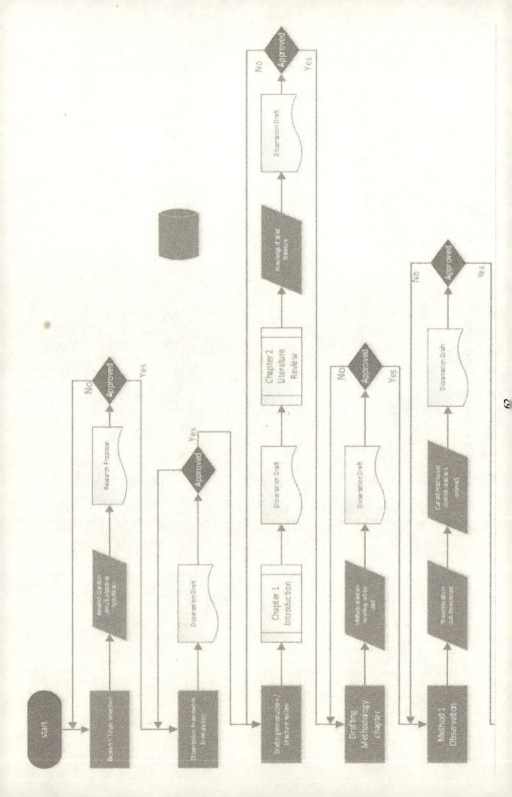

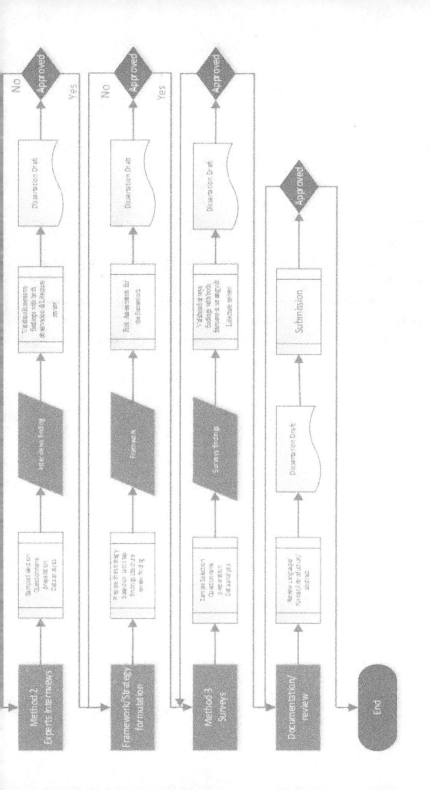

63

Appendix 2 – Interview Questions

Question 1: Does your organization interested in cloud computing? Give examples of current cloud services utilized?

Question 2: Is there any plan for the next 24 month for cloud computing adoption, especially for IaaS Cloud?

Question 3: What is the roles and responsibilities of your company in the cloud computing services and data in the cloud that are used?

Question 4: What do you think the difference in threat landscape between traditional IT and cloud computing?

Question 5: What are the current practice and controls that are used currently to protect data in the cloud?

Question 6: Is the current practice and controls are enough to protect the company assets in the cloud and encourage you for more cloud adoption?

Question 7: What is the role of the policies & procedures in protecting company assets in the cloud? Is different from what is used in Traditional IT?

Question 8: Do compliance and certificates encourage you in cloud adoption? If yes, How?

Appendix 3 – Interviews transcript

Interview 1

Interviewer	Haitham Ismail
Interviewee	A
Position/Years of Experience	System Engineer (Virtualization specialist) / 5 years
Date	March 12, 2018
Start	3:00 PM
End	3:10 PM
Location	Café

Haitham: *Would you mind introducing yourself to us, please?*

A: *yes sure, my name is A, I am 28 years old, I have completed like 5 years in IT field.*

Haitham: Does your organization interested in cloud computing? Give examples of current cloud services utilized?

A: yes of course, we are interested the cloud computing, everybody is interested I think, so we started using the cloud computing services since last 3 years. Currently our exchange server or our mailboxes in the cloud you are using the office 365 and we are planning to use more services in cloud as well.

Haitham: Is there any plan for the next 24 month for cloud computing adoption, especially for IaaS Cloud?

A: yes, off course. Actually, we have a plan, as we are planning to give or provide a cloud services to small and business currently. We are planning to give small business or startup companies cloud services. We are talking about storage and secure applications as well.

Haitham: What is your role in your company?

A: currently, I'm technical services engineer and my main roles is to go to other companies and implement new projects in different field like virtualizations, storage and servers from end to end.

Haitham: What is the roles and responsibilities of your company in the cloud computing services and data in the cloud that are used?

A: actually, we are planning in the near future to provide cloud services like we are planning to give the end users servers from end to end. We are going to provide computing services, storage, networking and we will be responsible to make them high available systems. So, we are talking about the hardware layer. We will be responsible for these staff.

Haitham: you mean the physical layer.

A: exactly, so the going to give the end user servers. They are going to install their applications on them. It is their call about the application, but we are going to be responsible for the underlying layer power, the networking and the resources.

Haitham: so, your customers will take care of the security of their applications.

A: exactly.

Haitham: What do you think the difference in threat landscape between traditional IT and cloud computing?

A: I believe cloud computing well be more secure from my point of view as the traditional IT cost more money and you have to do the maintenance and all these staff. So, from the customer point of view it will eliminate all these staff. Also, I'd like to add, in the traditional network. Especially for Startup Company, I do not think that they will invest in security and buying firewalls and all these staff related security to protect their data. So, when we are talking about providing cloud computing. So, We going to focusing on all these staff and we will make it very secure and we will invest more to make our customers comfortable and satisfied from security.

Haitham: What are the current practice and controls that are used currently to protect data in the cloud?

A: As I said that, I am service engineer but I think our network and security team going to focus on all of these staff so, also they are going to invest in securing the underlying layer in making all the system high available in terms of power, networking and availability. This is what I can say about this.

Haitham: what about confidentiality and integrity?

A: For sure, there are going to be an agreement about the classified information.

Haitham: Is the current practice and controls are enough to protect the company assets in the cloud and encourage you for more cloud adoption?

A: yes, for sure as I said we are going to focus on the startup company and small business and I don't think that these companies will invest in security and buying hardware for protection. So, they will be comfortable for cloud systems when they see our investment in the security and buying hardware from leader company to protect their servers and protect the data.

Haitham: What is the role of the policies & procedures in protecting company assets in the cloud conputing? Is different from what is used in Traditional IT?

A: for sure, when are talking about moving from traditional IT to cloud computing so we are talking about new risk, even though when cloud computing is more secure comparing to the traditional IT. But, I think there should be policies from both side cloud side and the customer side as well

Haitham: Do compliance and certificates encourage you in cloud adoption? If yes, How?

A: off course, when I see the other side is certified and he knows what he do with the systems that he provide, I will be more comfortable with working with them.

Haitham: you are talking regarding persons or organizations?

A: both of them actually, if I see that the company and their reputation is good so I will be more comfortable to deal with them.

Haitham: Thank you

A: no problem.

Interview 2

Interviewer	Haitham Ismail
Interviewee	B
Position/Years of Experience	Network Engineer (Firewall/Switching/Routing specialist) / 5 years
Date	March 14, 2018
Start	10:00 PM
End	10:10PM
Location	Telephone

Haitham: Do you mind to introduce yourself to us please?

B: yeah sure, my name is B; I am working as a network engineer in Bupa Arabia for five years of experience.

Haitham: the first question in our interview is, Is your organization is interested in cloud computing? And give us examples if so?

B: we are interested because mainly cloud computing will reduce costs for us and we will enhance the operation efficiency overall. Right now, we are having our colocation services hosted with the ISPs and we are thinking to expand it in future.

Haitham: your colocation you mean the disaster recovery site?.

B yes, it is a disaster recovery.

Haitham: is there any plan for the next 24 months for cloud computing adoption? Especially we are talking here regarding IaaS cloud.

B: yeah, actually the current cloud that we are adopted is already hosted with the ISP. The currently hosted services is based on Tier three services, and we are thinking to move to another colocation with tier four datacenter.

Haitham: what are the roles and responsibilities of your company in the cloud computing services that are being used?

B: Regarding the responsibilities, the cloud services is based on colocation and this location is shared with other companies, so our responsibility is to make sure that our racks are secured. We have our own cages and the responsibility of that area are completely for us. In addition to that off course, we are maintaining data security through firewalls. This is mainly our responsibility here the physical access to the racks and protections through the firewalls. The ISP is also securing the whole building through physical security and CCTV cameras and fire alarm control system and all other stuff like redundant power supply.

Haitham: What do you think the difference in Threat landscape between traditional IT and cloud computing?

B: okay, when we talk about threat difference here. Actually the cloud computing. It is much better about the service continuity because they are much better in the infrastructure readiness. They have different sources of links, redundancy in power. All the kind of services, which keep services online all the time. In the other side, in the traditional IT, the data will be more secure and safe because the data will be stored in our data center and our premises.

Haitham: what are the current practice and controls that are used currently to protect company data in cloud?

B: they are providing redundancy in the links and power. And they have the physical security 24/7. Also, they have CCTV cameras and they firewall. This is in the physical side and they are much better. Also, they have all measures that are applied by tier 3 data cloud hosting.

Haitham: what are the controls that are applied by your company in cloud?

B: we are putting the racks in cages. This our part in physical security and appliying much tighter firewall policies from firewall side.

Haitham: is the current practice and controls enough for protecting company assets in cloud and encourage other customers to join cloud era?

B: I think it is enough. And the controls measured depend on the tier of cloud computing, standard being followed. Right now, in my opinion, it is enough. But it will take time for moving from the traditional IT to cloud computing as it is a new technology and people are not touching it. Because the data now is hosted somewhere else. And it is hosted outside of company premises

Haitham: What is the role of the policies & procedures in protecting company assets in the cloud? Is different from what is used in Traditional IT?

B: I think different from what is used from traditional IT. Cloud computing, for sure, needs more policies and procedure to protect company data in cloud just to guarantee for companies that data are secured and you can trust them. For example, it could say data should be regularly backed up and service is accessible all the time.

Haitham: Do compliance and certificates encourage you in cloud adoption? If yes. How?

B: yeah of course, more certificates and compliance means more security measures. The main concern here is the security of the data. I think more certificate and compliance means more security measures

Haitham: Thank you Mr B

B: Any time

Interview 3

Interviewer	Haitham Ismail
Interviewee	C
Position/Years of Experience	Security Engineer (Firewall/Wireless specialist) / 6.5 years
Date	March 17, 2018
Start	00:15 AM
End	00:30 AM
Location	Telephone

Haitham: Would you please introduce yourself?

<u>C</u>: okay, my name is C. I start working in Saudi Arabia almost six years ago. I have experience of six and half years almost. I am responsible for security and wireless in my company

Haitham: Does your organization interested in cloud? And if so, please give examples of current cloud services utilized by your company?

<u>C</u>: yeah, off course everybody now a day is interested in the cloud computing services. It is the latest, so yeah we are very interested and we have multiple examples. For example, first of all, we as a company or even individuals we use cloud services, for example, dropbox, and also Gmail storage and these kinds of things. And as people now are going towards cloud so some as us and all the people we are trying to publish our services on the cloud and use the cloud services

So the most important example is IaaS. We are using Amazon AWS and we are hosting their cloud our CRM. So, basic start, It is a replication of our CRM. So, you know they provide us with a virtual infrastructure and you manage the virtual machines and our applications. It is very important as I somehow as CRM DR in cloud.

Haitham: Is there any plan for the next 24 months for cloud computing adoption, especially, we are talking here regarding IaaS cloud?

<u>C</u>: yeah, so, for instance, we are now a day, we are not investing any more on a physical hardware on datacenter. So we are trying to increase our services, we are trying to move them on cloud. So we are going more into hosting our services in the cloud. Especially in IaaS because we will have the ability to manage our virtual machines in IaaS, not like the past. So now we planning to move a replica of our domain controllers and even we trying to manage the FTP service that we have for a replication also and until now we will just do this replications and try to test basically in deep this new technology regarding the logs and management. And if everything goes okay with us, I think us and everybody like most of the

people to move to the cloud for not the very critical services but many things can be replicated outside without any compromise to their security and their environment.

Haitham: what are the roles and responsibilities of your company in the cloud computing services and data in cloud that are used?

C: okay, so basically, Infrastructure as a service. They only provide, as you know as a virtual environment. So we are responsible for installing the operating system. And doing the security patches and updating. And even updating and implementing a firewall virtual machine and antivirus and doing all the security policies, applying all the antimalware and IPS services on this virtual machine to protect all the data and the servers. However, for the platform and the server that we have, the cloud provider is responsible for maintenance so he does all the patching and antivirus update. However, we also requested to have a firewall virtual machine to increase our security. And even to proxy all the data between the servers for the inbound and the outbound traffic.

Haitham: what do you think the difference in threat landscape between traditional IT and Cloud computing?

C: Regarding traditional which means the services, which are on-premises. We have threats that are coming from inside and outside. From the inside, for instance the user attacks coming from USB, emails and even attacks from social engineering. For outside threats, such as DDOS attacks and hacking. Everything So on-preemies, they facing and they are compromised by all the attack. However, on the cloud, we are only dealing with the cloud sets and the cloud provider is the first line of defense. We are dealing only with the attacks performed on the cloud on the internet, which are DDOS attacks and these kind of advanced attacks. So the main difference is that we can exclude the inside attacks when we go to cloud and only deal with outside attacks which will be protected between our provider and security of our virtual machine on cloud.

A very important point is that because this cloud is a shared infrastructure and shared storage. So if for example our subscription expired and somebody else will take control of this infrastructure that you have which means the storage the most important thing. he will override information in your data. So in some way, there is a possibility that he will be able to extract your old data because it was already consumed by somebody else. So there is a problem here regarding the accessing the old data. That is a very important point the provider must escalate and be very clear how can they solve these problem

Haitham: what are the current practices and controls that are used to protect company data in cloud?

C: okay regarding our protection for the cloud. First, we are always updating the antivirus, which are on the cloud, and always patching the entire security platform on the operating systems. And for the main protection that we have, we are always implementing at least two firewall virtual machines we go for the new firepower from Cisco and paloalto virtual machine. Both of them, we have full license for cisco firepower, which are IPS, and Palo Alto is firepower. So, the traffic passes two layers of virtual machines firewalls and we are always checking the logs to check if any we missed anything. Basically, that is the thing that we are doing and until now we are safe

Haitham: Is the current practice and controls are enough to protect the company assets in the cloud and encourage you for more cloud adoption?

C: regarding is the practice and controls is enough. So basically and for instance, when the services are on premises we have more flexibility to implement different types of physical security and datacenter firewalls, perimeter firewall and IPS. Even cloud security that monitor our traffic like DNS umbrella to protect our DNS request. In premises, we have more flexibility regarding our security solution. However, for computing cloud, we are only limited to virtual machines that we can do and the kind of security that we can implement on the operating system. So, we don't have full flexibility in the cloud. until now we are not 100% encouraged to move more into the cloud until it is fully more tested and we are assure that no body will compromise our assets in the cloud. if this cloud business continually be safe for couple of extra years, I think that we and other people will invest more in the cloud.

Haitham: What is the roles of polices and procdure in protecting company assets in cloud? is it different from what is used in traditional IT?

C: Okay, so basically, once we are dealing with cloud and visualized environment so all the solution will be as a virtual solutions and regarding the virtual solutions there always be somehow small limitations rather than the physical limitations. So kind of the policies in general are the same but there is small different in the approach. However, the traditional security protection, because it is physical there are always more flexibility and it comes with more policies and produces to protect by adding multiple layers that we can use and they are already purchased. So it is somehow different.

Haitham: Do compliance and certificate encourage you in cloud adoption? And if yes, please tell us How?

C: so basically, we are always search for the compliance and certicate wise to test and meet our rules. Regarding the cloud provider, once they provide us for their compliance and how there datacenter are? For example, we have data disaster recovery for all our services, so, we will ensure that we will not lose all our data in cloud. That benefit us and encourage us. And because they can grantee for us that they can comply with the standard that we are forced in our country to follow (e.g data loss, ability to gain the logs and monitor and analyze the data) that will encourage of time and time consuming tasks to manage our services. So in a couple of years and now a days, because the provider become more comply to the policies we are encourage to do that.

Haitham: Thank you Mr, C it is been a pleasure have you in this interview

C: Thank you very much

Interview 4

Interviewer	Haitham Ismail
Interviewee	D
Position (Skills) /Years of Experience	Security Consultant (Firewall /Management/ Audit/ Compliance) / 16 years
Date	March 18, 2018
Start	01:15 PM
End	01:30 PM
Location	Telephone

Haitham: Could you please introduce yourself?

D: My name is D, I am a security practioner working in the field for 16 years now and I worked for a security consultant for many companies here and right now for one of the government organizations in Saudi Arabia.

Haitham: Does your organization interested in cloud computing? And If so, please give us examples?

D: yes, our organization is started to show interest in cloud computing, before it was not. Recently, from past one year it started interests. We started to have our email services hosted to the cloud "Microsoft Cloud".

Haitham: Is there any plan for the next 24 month for cloud computing adoption, especially for IaaS Cloud?

D: yes, it is in the plan actually, there is plan from the government itself to have take all the engineers and gather all the interties like all the departments and we will have a single data center or cloud for the ministry. But we will not used a third party like Amazon or Microsoft. We will use our own cloud and have all cloud PaaS, SaaS and IaaS.

Haitham: What is the roles and responsibilities of your company in protecting company data in cloud?

D: the cloud data is more risky for the attacks and everything. So, the responsibility increases now because sharing the load now between us and the cloud service provider. The current email service what we have hosted, the responsibilities is shared now with the cloud service provider. The data is in the cloud, so, we have to increase our roles and effort like traditional IT is less. But the cloud, even, data is taken care by the service provider, the responsibilities increases like taken audits and cordenate to check everything is in the right place or not. So, it is increases.

Haitham: What do you think the difference in threat landscape between traditional IT and cloud computing?

D: the traditional IT you have more workload, and do much security but you are not exposed to the threat landscape also. Because, you are having small SMB nobody is targeting you. Cloud computing, the main problem is sharing of the resources with others companies. So, if others get compromised, there is a chances that your company data also have been compromised. So, even cloud computing is more secure, it has more risky than traditional IT.

Haitham: What are the current practice and controls that are used currently to protect data in the cloud?

D: we have ISO standards and we are working with companies that are hosting the cloud "the Service provide" to have data center that are derived from the ISO and we are making sure that all ISO check lists are matched every three month to make sure that all this practice and controls are in place and conducting audit ever six month.

Haitham: Is the current practice and controls are enough to protect the company assets in the cloud and encourage you for more cloud adoption?

D: yes, I think the cloud practice and controls are well established. It is started long back. It is started 10 years back and it is okay. So, it will encourages us more to go to cloud.

Haitham: What is the role of the policies & procedures in protecting company assets in the cloud? Is different from what is used in Traditional IT?

D: if as I said, the roles and responsibilities in the cloud is different. The responsibility is shared here. So, the traditional IT you take care of everything and you decide what you want. But In cloud computing, you have an agreement and you cannot do what you want with your service provider. So, yes it is different for sure and roles of the policies increases. We have to be more specific and we have to protect by policies and procedures that well define who will access the data. So this is what happened. There is a difference.

Haitham: Do compliance and certificates encourage you in cloud adoption? If yes, How?

D: yes for sure, the compliance now we have a third party company that give you compliance certificate that will give you confidence that you are secure. The compliance certificates is renewable so you have to be working on it. Yes, if it is for us and for everyone it will encourage us.

Interview 5

Interviewer	Haitham Ismail
Interviewee	E
Position/Years of Experience	Presales Engineer / (Cloud Computing/Security consulting/privacy) / 5 years
Date	March 26, 2018
Start	10:15 PM
End	10:30 PM
Location	Telephone

Haitham: Could you please introduce yourself?

E: Hi Haitham. My name is E. I work for ABC cloud computing. My organisations is purely into delivering services to our customer's in infrastructure as well as software as a service and platform as a service. I am form provisioning team. I understand customer requirement, facilitate the actual security requirement for the customer and layout the design as per as their business tangible and intangible assets. I work with the compliance team to deliver the compliance services as well as security audit, and data privacy requirement for our customers. I front end the customers as well as the customer team and the technical team to answer and facilitate their business strategic and technical term requirement. I have been with this company since 15 years and I am good experience in cloud security.

Haitham: Does your organization interested in cloud computing? And If so, please give us examples from current cloud services utilized by your company?

E: Yes, our organization is primarily into cloud computing as it deliver the services of SaaS and IaaS to our customers. We pretty close with our customers in provisioning the latest software, which are using in information security field to be used by our customers. Some of the good examples would be application for handling the salesforce as well as backend HR management system, backend accounting system. This is some of the SaaS that we deliver. In terms of Infrastructure, we also provide platform where the developer code and developing teams can execute their software as well as use underline database to utilize and improvise their current business from the layout point of view. We have dedicated SLAs to make sure that infrastructure and business are up all the time and we maintain as a part from the package business services that we offer to our customers.

Haitham: Is there any plan for the next 24 month for cloud computing adoption, especially for IaaS Cloud?

E: Yes, we do have. In fact, we have been observing our customer requirement in this region since last 2 years. And even though, in terms of the legal as well as compliance obligations customers, especially to SME to mid-level enterprise organization, are turning to the cloud who really want to save their operation as well as infrastructure cost in managing the cloud and the overall overhead in the TCO or capex and opex consumptions. So especially for IaaS, we have wide variety of different tier level of services that we are planning in the next 24 month as offering to our customer. We gonna start with some of the well-known mechanism by which customers offload their data to us. Customer can connect to our existing database server using their APIs and custom developed applications, which we may host in our premises. Also, customers can develop depending upon the infrastructure we are providing to them. We are providing backup and restore services to our customers in the cloud. so, this is what we are covering in the next 24 month and many other offer are going to be keep coming as we progress further with cloud computing and security infrastructure.

Haitham: What is the roles and responsibilities of your company in protecting company data in cloud?

E: since we start our job from the software layer, I think we understood the market requirement and the overall strategy in which the cloud computing is evolving, we start working back in the days when it was only purely a software services we were selling to our customers. We were offering software for managing the backend as well as HR Management system for the organizations in this region. But, compliance, regulations, and legal obligations are strengthen now a days and information security, privacy and the regulations are holding our customers a part, so we are working very very strictly to make sure that data privacy and customer information as well as sensitive details are always recorded and maintained with customer control. Customer can manage encryption. They can offload what kind of data privacy they want. We as a service provider, we even have a choose that literally no control on how data store on our storage making sure that customer have secure the information that they are saving. We playing a very deep role in maintaining our roles to ensure that customer's information is intact and it private to them. We do not have role to intervene about how the data is being stored. We do not have any visibility. So, we want make sure that our infrastructure is secure to provide a secure mechanism for data storage to our customers. Our channel to access the data is secure. Our medium for customers to maintain data privacy is open and independent and to insure customer's data is available all the times. So, these are the roles and responsibilities that we have aligned ourselves and we working with align with customer requirements.

Haitham: What do you think the difference in threat landscape between traditional IT and cloud computing?

E: Haitham as we see today, perimeter and the customer boundaries are dying. Users are not limited to the perimeter. So, customers are now a days wanting to be more mobile. So traditional IT system were well established and focused on having the punch of users and the logical group of users who binded and stored behind the perimeter. Today, if you look on the threats traditional IT, it was making sure, how the users work from all locations or multiple locations and how the information and data privacy can be maintained. But, when we talk cloud computing, the premitier is no longer a logical boundary or a physical boundary, it's pretty much anywhere you could be in the world. Now, that brings different level of threats. So, you only protect the perimeter when talk about securing the perimeter. In case of the cloud computing, it is pretty much about anywhere. The moment data leaks the organizations, you leave that perimeter boundary. The moment information leaks your machine; you literally leave that secure boundary and your machine how the information are going outside the boundary. So, privacy was the main concern whenever the traditional IT was compared with cloud computing as the information and the data is not in your control. It was easy to regularize when you are talking with securing your traditional IT and perimeter based boundary which was even today is difficult. From many vendor in cloud computing who are really welling to offer different services to our customers, but not everyone can ensure data privacy, not everyone can ensure quality of services which important to the customers. Many important things that would arise when customers talks about moving away from traditional IT to cloud computing. Service level agreement (SLA), when I looking for cloud services for a company what kind of service level of agreement I can have. What is the downtime and what is the business availability for me. So, I can look on maximum tolerable downtime or how do I calculate the overall risk for the information that is not there in my premises. So, in detailing and summary, privacy, medium of data storage, regularization, compliance, legal obligations and boundary based controls. Information might be in a different country, but may be my country do not want to do business with that country or may be having a trading barge. So, these kinds of obligation will always arise when we are talking between difference in traditional IT and cloud computing.

Haitham: What are the current practice and controls that are used currently to protect data in the cloud?

E: practice that I have seen today is maturing. Back in the days, when we look at the services they were really ad-hoc. Some of the vendors who started to offer the services as private cloud services. It was using controls that information were not only accessible for just everyone, but it is traditionally oriented to one a company. So, that is one way the threat landscape were reduced, secondly, we are talking about, secure mechanism to make sure that the channel were secure to access the data. Strong authentication to make sure that authorized access are controlled. Data encryption in the storage where information are stored for the customers and strong service level agreement in case a data breach or information disclosure the service provider are offering. A Compensation to their customers for highly sensitive information. These are some of the controls that are being used and nevertheless, this is not the end, this is just the beginning as cloud computing is evolving. But for my knowledge this actually how we are providing services to our customers and ensure having control to protect company data in cloud.

Haitham: Do you think that these current practice and controls are enough to protect the company assets in the cloud and encourage you for more cloud adoption?

E: there is no one control that is precise and strong enough to protect data in your perimeter or in your boundary or outside the cloud. As I said, cloud computing is evolving and its providing some benefits to the customers. The security of cloud is also evolving; nevertheless, this is not the end. At every span of information security life cycle, we see the threats are being identified so this is defiantly not enough. But, these controls are maturing and have enough capability to convince customers to move the data in the cloud considering the compliance and the regulations that are already there and as long as the service provider is welling to adhere to that.

Haitham: What is the role of the policies & procedures in protecting company assets in the cloud? Is different from what is used in Traditional IT?

E: I think policies and procedures plays a vital role when we are talking about protecting company data in the cloud. In fact, this is the hardline, which identified what I should trust, what I can depend on. So, defiantly policies and procedures plays a very important role. It could be about privacy, it could be about data protection. It could be legal and regulations. It is one documentation which talks about how I can depend on the basis of my decision to move my data in cloud. It is definitely quite different from traditional IT because your controls are inside your boundary. Your DMZ are inside your boundary. So, you are able to control what goes out and what comes in by physical, technical and logical controls. In case of cloud computer, the information is not in your perimeter control. So, the data center is hosted in different company. The information is laying somewhere. Today we are talking about content distribution network, so it could be anywhere. We are talking about software defined network so the information can take any channel. It can go through a country or geological boundary that is notat all in good relation with your company or your country. Yes, it is different in terms of type of controls, generality of controls, the visibility, the flexibility, and the content.

Haitham: Do compliance and certificate encourage you in cloud adoption? And if yes, please tell us How?

E: when I represent my company, I really do not feel the compliance and certification is real adoption. Business requirements and the focus of the organization and its dependency of operation and the total cost of ownership decide if I want to go and adopt cloud or not. Compliance and certificates is a thought that will give me additional comfort that I can depend on the cloud. So, my first level of exposure is my business requirement; my second level is how I get convinced to put my data and my information in cloud leaving my boundary and going to get stored in cloud on one of the servers which are on the internet cloud. so, there is some sort of encouragement but it is complementary not the only way to convince.

Haitham: Thank you Mr E

E: you are welcome Haitham

Appendix 4 – Surveys Questions

Cloud Security Infrastructure - New template to enhance security in the Middle East

Q.1. Do you think that you have full visibility for the security posture for your data in cloud and risks associated with it? (examples of risks: data lock-in, loss of governance, CSP malicious insiders, Insecure data deletion, management Interface compromises, Abused cloud services, Insecure APIs, Economic denial of service EDOS, etc.)

A1. Yes, I have complete visibility

A2. No, I do not have

A3. I have some concern, but I'm not aware the mentioned risks

Q2. Do you think that there is lack of security expertise in IT practitioners in the Region? Expertise: The availability of qualified cloud security practitioners (e.g. CCSP or CISSP certificate holders) and the lack of security knowledge for normal IT practitioners (e.g. developers, system admin, DBA admin, exchange admin, etc.)

A1. Yes, the qualified engineers are rarely to find

A2. No, the expertise is available

Q3. Does exists of a template for cloud security infrastructure can help you in protecting your cloud IaaS infrastructure? (This template will give you what to adopt, how to protect, and how to negotiate with cloud provider SLA)

A1 Yes, off course

A2 No, I do not need it

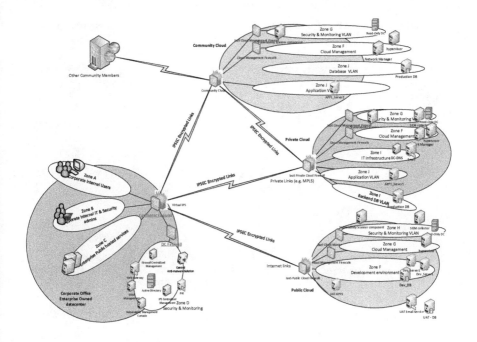

Q4. Do you think that Isolation is achieved in this template?

Firewalls isolate CSP Management, CS Management, CS Security & monitoring, CS IaaS in good architecture etc.

A1. Yes

A2. No

A3. Maybe

Q5. Do you think the below controls are enough to have full visibility on the security posture in all cloud deployments?

Security Controls	Description	Compliance Standard
Security Information and Event Monitoring (SIEM)	it collects, correlates and analyses logs generated from network and security nodes, operating systems and applications, besides, it generates reports that have full visibility on the organization security posture (Stephenson, 2014)	NIST 800-53 IR - 5
Vulnerability Management software	it scans the nodes for detecting missing patches, vulnerabilities or misconfigured settings and software (Kovács, et al., 2013), in general, it is consists of manager and scanner	NIST 800-53 RA - 5
Netflow Analyzer	it provides full visibility for all traffic that crosses the network node (e.g. Firewall) (Santos, 2015)	NIST 800-53 SI - 4
Asset Management software	Its main purpose to discover and have an inventory of all components of the organization's information systems within the authorized boundary (NIST, 2018a).	NIST 800-53 CM - 8
Identity Access Management Software (e.g. DC, RODC, etc.)	Active directory can be used to authenticate, authorize and account users and computer account (Melber, 2004).	NIST 800-53 IA - 2
Syslog Servers	It captures logs for analysis for previous period of time (Liu, 2009)	NIST 800-53 AU - 12
Reverse proxy servers/Anti-malware/ proxy servers	it helps in protection from malicious code that can be executed locally or from a remote place and have a direct impact on confidentiality, integrity and security (NIST, 2018b)	NIST 800-53 SI-3

A1. Yes

A2. No

A3. Maybe

Q6. Do you think that the distribution of data across different deployment models are effective?

Data sensitivity	Example	Deployment model
High	Medical records, customer information, trade secrets, trade secrets.	Private
Medium/High	Shared information due to regulations (e.g. some medical records that are shared between hospitals and government)	Community
Medium/Low	UAT environments, developing environments	Public

A1. Yes

A2. No

A3. Maybe

Q7. Do you think that the following Cloud management zone are enough for establishing control over IaaS Cloud Infrastructure?

(The blow table include IaaS cloud component for a VMware as an example (similar solution from other vendors might be included), CSP or CSs should have isolated similar cloud management zone)

Security Controls	Description
ESXi	Provides bare-metal virtualization of servers so you can consolidate your applications on less hardware.
vCenter Server	Provides a centralized platform for managing vSphere environments.
vCenter Site Recovery Manager	Provides disaster recovery capability that lets you perform automated orchestration and no disruptive testing for virtualized applications.
vRealize Automation	Provides functionality for deploying and provisioning of business-relevant cloud services across private and public clouds, physical infrastructure, hypervisors, and public cloud providers.
vRealize Automation Application Services	Provides automated application provisioning in the cloud including deploying and configuring the application's components and dependent middleware platform services on infrastructure clouds.
vRealize Business for vSphere	Provides transparency and control over the costs and quality of IT services that are critical for private or hybrid cloud success.
vRealize Configuration Manager	Provides automation of configuration and compliance management across your virtual, physical and cloud environments, assessing them for operational and security compliance.
vRealize Hyperic	Provides monitoring of operating systems, middleware and applications running in physical, virtual, and cloud environments.
vRealize Infrastructure Navigator	Provides automated discovery of application services, visualizes relationships, and maps dependencies of applications on virtualized compute, storage and network resources.
vRealize Orchestrator	Provides the capability to create workflows that automate activities such as provisioning a virtual machine, performing scheduled maintenance, initiating backups, and many others.
vRealize Operations Manager	Provides comprehensive visibility and insights into the performance, capacity and health of your infrastructure.
vSphere Big Data Extensions	Simplifies running Big Data workloads on the vSphere platform.
vSphere Data Protection	Provides advanced data protection with backup and recovery to disk.
vSphere Replication	Provides replication, at the individual virtual machine disk level, between data stores hosted on any storage.

A1. Yes

A2. No

A3. Maybe

Q8. Do you think using of Arch 4 enhance security, less restrictive model can be used?

Please refer to different Cloud Arch models in the below table

	VM Images At Rest	VM Migration	CSP Sys-admin IAM	Data Center physical security	Hypervisor, BIOS, CPU	VM Isolation	Tenant IAM	App. White-listing
Cloud Arch 1	Not encrypted	Unencrypted memory pages and packets	Single factor	All CSP employees have access	HV, BIOS not signed CPU without TPM	No network, CPU isolation	Single factor	No
Cloud Arch 2	Not encrypted	Unencrypted memory pages and packets	2 factor—time limited token code	CSP employee access limited & controlled + USB server ports disabled	HV, BIOS not signed CPU without TPM	No network, CPU isolation	Single factor	No
Cloud Arch 3	Not encrypted	Unencrypted memory pages and packets	2 factor—time limited token code	CSP employee access limited & controlled + USB server ports disabled	HV, BIOS not signed CPU without TPM	No network, CPU isolation	2 factor—time limited token	No
Cloud Arch 4	Encrypted at rest – file access monitoring	Encrypted memory pages and packets	2 factor—time limited token code	CSP employee access limited & controlled+ USB server ports disabled	Signed HV, signed BIOS CPU with TPM	Virtual PANs, temporal CPU isolation	2 factor—time limited token	Yes

A1. Yes

A2. No

A3. Maybe

Q9. Do you think that following these template will help you in securing your data in different cloud deployments model?

A1. Yes

A2. No

A3. Maybe

Q10. Do you think that Isolation is achieved in this template? (Isolation between CSP management, CSP security & monitoring, CS IaaS cloud, CS management and CS Security and monitoring zones)

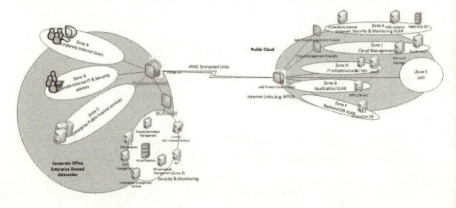

A1. Yes

A2. No

A3. Maybe

Q11. Do you think the below controls are enough to have full visibility on the security posture in Public cloud?

Security Controls	Description	Compliance Standard
Security Information and Event Monitoring (SIEM)	it collects, correlates and analyses logs generated from network and security nodes, operating systems and applications, besides, it generates reports that have full visibility on the organization security posture (Stephenson, 2014)	NIST 800-53 IR - 5
Vulnerability Management software	it scans the nodes for detecting missing patches, vulnerabilities or misconfigured settings and software (Kovács, et al., 2013), in general, it is consists of manager and scanner	NIST 800-53 RA - 5
Netflow Analyzer	it provides full visibility for all traffic that crosses the network node (e.g. Firewall) (Santos, 2015)	NIST 800-53 SI - 4
Asset Management software	Its main purpose to discover and have an inventory of all components of the organization's information systems within the authorized boundary (NIST, 2018a).	NIST 800-53 CM - 8
Identity Access Management Software (e.g. DC, RODC, etc.)	Active directory can be used to authenticate, authorize and account users and computer account (Melber, 2004).	NIST 800-53 IA - 2
Syslog Servers	It captures logs for analysis for previous period of time (Liu, 2009)	NIST 800-53 AU - 12
Reverse proxy servers/Anti-malware/ proxy servers	it helps in protection from malicious code that can be executed locally or from a remote place and have a direct impact on confidentiality, integrity and security (NIST, 2018b)	NIST 800-53 SI-3

A1. Yes

A2. No

A3. Maybe

Q12. Do you think that the distribution of data across public cloud deployment are effective?

Data sensitivity	Example	Deployment model
High/Medium/Low	Most of the companies data	Private
Medium/High	Shared information due to regulations (e.g. some medical records that are shared between hospitals and government)	Community

A1. Yes

A2. No

A3. Maybe

Q13. Do you see any deference in cloud management zone components of different cloud deployment?

Security Controls	Description
ESXi	Provides bare-metal virtualization of servers so you can consolidate your applications on less hardware.
vCenter Server	Provides a centralized platform for managing vSphere environments.
vCenter Site Recovery Manager	Provides disaster recovery capability that lets you perform automated orchestration and no disruptive testing for virtualized applications.
vRealize Automation	Provides functionality for deploying and provisioning of business-relevant cloud services across private and public clouds, physical infrastructure, hypervisors, and public cloud providers.
vRealize Automation Application Services	Provides automated application provisioning in the cloud including deploying and configuring the application's components and dependent middleware platform services on infrastructure clouds.
vRealize Business for vSphere	Provides transparency and control over the costs and quality of IT services that are critical for private or hybrid cloud success.
vRealize Configuration Manager	Provides automation of configuration and compliance management across your virtual, physical and cloud environments, assessing them for operational and security compliance.
vRealize Hyperic	Provides monitoring of operating systems, middleware and applications running in physical, virtual, and cloud environments.
vRealize Infrastructure Navigator	Provides automated discovery of application services, visualizes relationships, and maps dependencies of applications on virtualized compute, storage and network resources.
vRealize Orchestrator	Provides the capability to create workflows that automate activities such as provisioning a virtual machine, performing scheduled maintenance, initiating backups, and many others.
vRealize Operations Manager	Provides comprehensive visibility and insights into the performance, capacity and health of your infrastructure.
vSphere Big Data Extensions	Simplifies running Big Data workloads on the vSphere platform.
vSphere Data Protection	Provides advanced data protection with backup and recovery to disk.
vSphere Replication	Provides replication, at the individual virtual machine disk level, between data stores hosted on any storage.

A1. Yes

A2. No

A3. Maybe

Q14. Please write your feedback on templates offered and recommending for future enhancement